IRRATIONAL EXUB...
The Myth of the Cel...

ABOUT THE AUTHOR

ANTHONY SWEENEY is an independent investment analyst. A native of Limerick, he received his MBA from Edinburgh Business School at Heriot-Watt University. An expert on European financial markets, he currently resides in Germany and the USA. His previous books include *Strategic Implications of [European] Monetary Union.*

Irrational Exuberance
The Myth of the Celtic Tiger

Anthony Sweeney

BLACKHALL
Publishing

BLACKHALL PUBLISHING
26 Eustace Street
Dublin 2
Ireland

e-mail: blackhall@tinet.ie

ISBN: 1 901657 84 1

A catalogue record for this book is available
from the British Library.

Printed in Ireland by
Betaprint

Contents

Introduction vii

1. A Primer in Economics 1
2. The Business Cycle 15
3. The Wrong Rate 25
4. Straining at the Seams 35
5. Consumer Psychology 47
6. Boomtown 59
7. Credit 69
8. The Housing Market 77
9. Analogies 91
10. The State of the World 99
11. European Monetary Union 107
12. Chronology of Recession 125
13. Analysis and Adaptation for Consumers 139
14. Analysis and Adaptation for Business 149
15. Silver Lining 159

Conclusion 165

Bibliography 169

Introduction

I wrote this book in order to alert people to the danger of a down-turn in the economy. This is an extremely difficult task to achieve in the face of the irrational exuberance being expressed by nearly every sector of our economy. It is still, however, a warning that must be sounded.

The Irish economy has moved in the last three years from controlled productive growth, to uncontrollable and irrational growth. Our newspaper headlines triumph our economic success, the streets of Dublin are awash with money, consumers are spending wildly and everyone expects the good times to last forever. Unfortunately, they will not. Ireland, and Dublin in particular, is experiencing a classic economic 'boom/bust' cycle and one of the most insidious facets of such an economic event, is that it is extremely difficult to convince anyone that the boom portion of it will end. The general consensus, contrary to every historical analogy and economic theory, is that it will last forever. Such beliefs, eventually, even extend into the highest corridors of power, as our politicians begin to believe the unbelievable. One of the many consequences of such beliefs is near reckless financial behaviour on the behalf of consumers. Furthermore, anyone who attempts to offer a contrary position or suggest restraint is accused of 'doom and gloom' economics and 'begrudgery'.

In spite of this, I feel I can demonstrate the origins of our economic problems, the clear signals that the economy is in the boom phase of a boom/bust cycle, the route the recession will take and, more importantly, the proactive measures people can take to protect themselves. It would not be sufficient for me to predict a recession without suggesting practical financial measures that consumers and businesses can take to insulate themselves.

The tone of this book, while urging strong caution, is ultimately positive because I firmly believe that anyone that is forewarned is forearmed. I also discuss the immense opportunities that I believe will be available during an economic downturn in Ireland. Every cloud has a silver lining, and for those with patience, that lining may even be golden.

Some people may find it strange that I am writing a book about the Irish economy when I do not live in Ireland at the moment. Paradoxically however, this is why I feel qualified to write this book. I have a certain amount of clinical detachment from my native country, which allows me to see what others in the midst of the boom cannot. I visit Ireland regularly and it was during these frequent trips that I witnessed, incrementally, what others were, I believe, seeing gradually. Slowly, visit by visit, I saw Dublin turn into the London of the late-1980s. I lived in London during this period and, ultimately, witnessed the consequences of the economic downturn that happened there.

While writing this book, I tried to avoid the normal tendency of economic books to be turgid and complex. I believe I have achieved this and produced a book that balances explanation with illumination. Economics is essentially a simple subject, it is just made complex by over-analysis. Economics is, after all, the only area where two people can win Noble prizes for saying the opposite thing. The economic theory, which is included, is written in a relaxed, but not simplistic style, and, hopefully, it will be useful in all aspects of your life not just in the context of this subject. I hope you find this work enjoyable and informative.

The structure of this book is fairly straightforward. The first two chapters introduces some basic economic theories that are essential to a complete understanding of the overall work. I believe it is important to build the foundation initially, as too much explanation later on can cloud matters. From Chapter 3 to 8, I demonstrate how the excessive growth is plainly visible in Ireland, and the affect this is having on consumers.

From Chapter 9 to 12, I discuss how I believe this boom will play out, and use analogies and theory to support my arguments. The remainder of the book is taken up with a demonstration with how consumers and businesses can best deal with any downturn, and how some people can even gain from it.

Anthony Sweeney
March 1999

For Togora

A Primer in Economics

The age of chivalry is gone. That of sophisters,
economists and calculators has succeeded;
and the glory of Europe is extinguished forever.

Edmund Burke

The above quotation probably represents what most people think about economics and economists. Economics was also once described as, "the dismal science"; hopefully I can go some way towards correcting this misconception. Economics is not only interesting, but it is also highly relevant to every aspect of our lives. Economics is often confused with accounting or finance; but it has little to do with balance sheets or cash flow projections. Economics is, at its core, about people. People have needs and wants, but there are limited resources in the world to satisfy them. The realisation that wants are infinite and resources are finite, leads to many conflicts. Economics revolves around illustrating the various options available to consumers, businesses, governments and, sometimes, societies as a whole. While this may all sound rather mundane, economics can explore many curious and fascinating issues to gain a better understanding of human nature, and how we interact with the world around us.

The role of this chapter is to lay an explanatory groundwork for many other topics in the book, by explaining some basic economic theory. The areas I want to look at are:
- supply and demand;
- efficient markets;
- economies of scale;
- specialisation;
- international trade;
- money and banks;
- speculation;
- the cobweb theorem.

SUPPLY AND DEMAND

Supply and demand is a basic economic concept that is the bed-rock upon which most of our economies rest. Every single product or service in our economy is demanded by one party and supplied by another at a mutually agreed price. Hence, we have the three factors in the equation: the quantity demanded, the quantity supplied and the price.

Demand usually creates supply – if I walked into a large supermarket in Dublin and cleared the shelves of smoked salmon, they would probably be filled again within hours. If 200 people walked into every supermarket in Dublin and cleared the shelves of smoked salmon and then demanded more from the overworked manager, he would have to find it. He would call the supplier, who would call the fish farm, who would respond to such demand. It may take a couple of months or longer but supply would respond to a consistently larger demand for smoked salmon. This is the beautiful efficiency of our consumer society – demand by consumers is met by increased supply from producers, who are eager to make a profit – and everyone is happy.

But let's stop for a moment and use the analogy to its fullest; what would happen to the salmon market in Dublin in between the increase in demand and the compensating increase in supply from fish farms? During this period we would see another facet of the interplay between supply and demand. With more demand than supply, the supermarket could raise the price of salmon. As the price rose, consumers may re-evaluate their desire for salmon and may not buy it, eventually demand and supply would be matched perfectly, at a higher price. The above example demonstrates two simple rules. The first one is that price is a function of supply and demand conditions, this means that price is a result of, or derived from, supply and demand levels. Written in mathematical short hand it is expressed:

$$price = f \text{ (supply, demand).}$$

The second rule is that, if supply is fixed, or almost fixed, and it takes time to increase it substantially, for example the salmon, then we can remove supply from the picture and price will be a function solely of demand:

$$price = f \text{ (demand).}$$

Supply and demand rules apply no matter what you are dealing with, it is at the heart of all transactions. The Boeing company makes jet planes and they are bound by the same rules of demand and supply as supermarkets selling salmon.

If Boeing has more buyers than they have 747s, then it can raise the price. If the world's airlines are not prospering, then they will not need many new planes and so demand will be weak. If Boeing wants to sell their jets in this kind of market, they will have to reduce the price to entice airlines to reconsider their decision, and so raise demand. They will probably be a little bit more sophisticated in how they do it than the fishmonger, but, basically, it is the same action.

Auctions are a good example of supply and demand in operation. In an auction, the supply is fixed at one item, the price is then raised slowly until there is only one remaining bidder and hence demand now also equals one. (Diverting for a moment to a tangential issue, it could be pointed out that auctions create a paradoxical situation. The person who ends up 'winning' at auction is stuck with a very annoying situation known as the winner's curse. Economists would point out that he was the only person in the room who thought this item was worth what he paid for it. Probability dictates that there are probably richer and wiser people in the room and every single one of those thought the price paid was too high, otherwise they would have surpassed the bid. The 'winner' of the auction is left with the worrying thought, "What did they know about the item that I didn't?" This is a very discomforting thought, which also has economic significance as we will see later.)

EFFICIENT MARKETS

Markets are simply places where buyers and sellers meet, it could be on Moore Street or Wall Street, both have equal claim to the title 'efficient market'. In fact, I could put up an extremely strong argument that Moore Street is the most efficient. Yet what exactly defines an efficient market? An efficient market is where buyers and sellers are free to exchange products and where each is in possession of 'perfect' information. This simple definition carries with it great significance, because it leads to what is known as the efficient market mechanism theory.

This theory is simple but potent – it states that the price for which something is sold in a market, reflects all the information known about that product at the time of sale. If you hear on the radio this morning that Smurfit is going to have an excellent year, you may be inclined to purchase its shares. However, it is not worth your while as everyone now knows this information, and the price will almost immediately reflect it. Other investors with near instantaneous response times will have bid up the share price before your hand reaches your mobile phone. The share price on any stock exchange is simply the last price at which those shares were traded between two people on the floor of the exchange. So, in the case of Smurfit, there is no point buying those shares as the good information is already priced into the price. This phrase 'priced into' is significant because it indicates that the price is not just a number, but a store of information concerning the product. The price of something is the result of vast amounts of interactions that have been brought together into one small number. Nobody actually sits down and manually does this, the invisible automatic interactions of the market creates it. Communism failed because communists always presumed they could replicate the market mechanism and assign prices to items. This was never possible because it is simply impossible to calculate constantly the near infinite and continuous interactions of all market participants.

There is, however, one significant flaw with the efficient market mechanism hypotheses, which is that information may not be available equally to the various market participants. In many situations, the buyer may know more about the product than the seller or vice versa, and this causes distortions. In technical terms, you could say that information distribution was unsymmetrical, rather than symmetrical. In more practical terms, there was an unsymmetrical information distribution problem when I bought my first car. The salesman selling it to me knew the engine would be lucky to make it off the forecourt, I, on the other hand, did not know this fact. Those with perfect knowledge about something will probably make rational decisions, those without may possibly make irrational ones. Governments strive in many cases to make information symmetrical, which is why practices, such as insider trading, are illegal. If it was not, then vast fortunes could be made by company executives at the expense of those buying and selling that company's shares simply because they could act on information before it was in the public domain.

ECONOMIES OF SCALE

Let's start with a simple question: why does the price of news-papers in Ireland cost significantly more than the price in the UK or the USA. *The Irish Times* costs £0.85 and the London *Times* costs less than half of this, as do most American papers. The simple reason is economies of scale – the more newspapers you produce, the cheaper each extra paper becomes. Let's take some hypothetical figures and assume it costs £30,000 to pay the re-porters, editors and whatever other costs are necessary to get a daily newspaper ready for printing. These costs we will call fixed, because they cannot be changed in the short-term. No matter how many copies of a paper are printed, these will still be fixed costs and must be paid. Now, if the paper expects to sell only 100,000 copies, then only that number will be printed, and each one of these will have to carry its share of the fixed costs of £30,000. This would work out at £0.30 per newspaper, i.e. £30,000 divided by 100,000 copies. Yet a paper that expected to sell one million copies, would have a fixed cost per newspaper of only £0.03 each, i.e. £30,000 divided by one million copies. There are also other costs of producing a paper, namely paper, electricity and ink, to mention the major ones. Let's say these total up to £0.10 per issue. These costs are known as variable costs as they obviously vary with the number of papers produced. So the final cost of a newspaper is equal to the fixed cost it has to bear plus the variable costs. In the case of the hypothetical newspaper that prints 100,000 copies then, the cost of produc-tion will be £0.30 + £0.10, which is £0.40 per paper. In the case of the newspaper with the larger circulation, it will be £0.03+ £0.10, which is £0.13 per paper. These are significant cost ad-vantages for the latter paper.

To move things back to reality now. The London *Times* has a potential market of up to 1 million people, and *The Irish Times* has a potential sales figure of probably only 100,000-200,000 copies.

Economies of scale dictates that no matter what *The Irish Times* does, its price will always be significantly higher. There is simply no way of shaking off the high fixed costs of running a quality newspaper for a small market. Those who buy the paper are willing to accept this and pay the price accordingly.

This rule applies in varying degrees to practically all goods produced. This is why most goods produced for larger markets, such as the US, are significantly cheaper than for smaller markets. The ability to produce large quantities for one homogenous audience will allow the final price to be extremely low.

Economies of scale also explain why our modern society tends to centralise production in large factories. The more one factory produces, then the cheaper each item is – there is nothing to be achieved by breaking up factories into smaller entities. Henry Ford demonstrated this well. The more Model Ts he produced, the cheaper each one became on average. Mr Ford took standardisation to the extremes with his famous phrase, "You can have any colour, as long as it is black." Every Model T was black, he would not even alter the production line to allow a different colour to be applied as it would drive up the costs. Mr Ford also demonstrated the advantages of another economic principle known as 'specialisation'.

SPECIALISATION

Specialisation is a corollary of economies of scale. It refers to the gains produced from one person continually doing one task, which they have mastered. In its most micro of forms, this results in production lines. One worker putting part A on to part B all day long, will become extremely efficient and quick. If you break production up into a series of such steps, then overall production will become extremely efficient. The first person to realise this was Adam Smith, but the first industrialist to take it to its 'natural' conclusion was Henry Ford. Ford realised that 1,000 men doing one-thousandth of the work of making a car, could make more cars than 1,000 men all individually attempting to assemble a car on their own. Equal amounts of man-hours would occur in both cases, but with specialisation in production lines, a far greater number of cars would be produced. This concept is now globally accepted, although in his time it was fairly revolutionary. The great triumph of his efforts was to reduce the price of a car so dramatically that the 'common man' could afford it. This was a significant and critical point in the formation of our modern societies. Mass production enabled the working and middle classes to afford what had previously been the preserve of the wealthy.

INTERNATIONAL TRADE

International trade is the macro version of specialisation. It is only logical that if each person should specialise, then so should each country. For example, France has many advantages in producing wine over Ireland – climate, a long history of viniculture, and the right soil to name but a few. If we produced wine, it would cost much more per bottle than it does in France. So we are happy to let France produce the wine, and then purchase their surplus from them. Thus, economies of scale and specialisation combine to produce gains from trade for all of us. Each country has advantages which allows it to produce certain goods and services more efficiently than others. They may then trade their excess production with other countries, so that everyone gains. Sometimes a country may have a natural monopoly, such as oil, diamonds or coal, in other cases, a country may be devoid of any natural benefits and may just have an inherent expertise. Many of these inherent advantages may be difficult to explain but they just exist and we accept them. Why is so much car production centred in Japan? We could spend half this book trying to figure this out, but we just accept it. Japan has no oil, no coal, and almost no other natural resources but it has an inherent, almost cultural, ability to organise resources in such a way as to produce many consumer goods extremely efficiently.

Ireland is a small country, and we have finally realised, after years of futile effort, that we cannot compete with larger countries in certain areas of industry where they have massive economies of scale in production. In the past, Ireland spent much time, and resources, attempting to make the production of steel, cars and other such goods profitable. It was simply an exercise in futility. The advantages of specialisation are such that the Japanese or the British can make cars cheaper and ship them to us. However, to name one small example, we have many beautiful golf courses that are so inexpensive relative to Tokyo, that the Japanese are willing to fly half-way around the world to use them. We trade our surplus supply of golf-courses for Japan's surplus supply of cars. This creates the maximum amount of utility for all.

Much time and money has been wasted by governments 'protecting' industries from competition, simply because these industries were in marginal constituencies or had vocal business interests supporting them. It has been proved numerous times that imposing embargoes, tariffs, and duties are a waste of resources and penalise the citizens of a country. In recent years, the World Trade Organisation (previously GATT) has led the way in helping countries to drop barriers to free trade. The more we trade our surpluses, the more every country benefits. It is true that in a minority of cases, people will suffer, but it is a case of the benefit to the vast majority outweighing the special interests of a small minority. Utopia does not exist.

Ireland prospers now because it abandoned 'old' industries and embraced new ones in which we can compete effectively.

We have many advantages that may not appear as specialisations but in fact are. Tourism, location, language, regulatory environment, human resources, all of these are advantages with which we can differentiate ourselves. For example, it may seem obvious, but no other country in the world can offer a holiday in Ireland. When you combine this with the fact that 40 or 50 million Americans claim Irish ancestry, the possibilities for the tourist industry are significant. Tourism is a relatively clean industry which distributes money and employment throughout the country evenly. Another 'natural' advantage we have in Ireland, is an educated workforce that speaks English. With the advent of sophisticated and cheap communication, there is demand for such people by American companies for interactive telephone services. This is not solely because such labour is in short supply in the US, but because the Irish speak a relatively pure form of English and our accents are such that we are easily understood by people from nearly every region in the US. The same cannot be said for many Americans, who tend to have strong regional variations in their accents.

Overall it is much easier to conduct trade when you are free to export to whomever you want, and the government allows its citizens to import what they want. Complex customs system waste needless resources trying to force populations to consume a more expensive indigenous variety of some product. Equal amounts of resources are wasted by consumers trying to circumvent these systems.

Unfortunately, no matter how easy it is to prove the advantages of free trade, many countries still attempt to subvert it. The main reasons is, of course, politicians. Politicians' primal instinct is to stay in office, and they know that they are elected locally not internationally. 'Keep jobs in Ireland' or Germany or France or America is a very powerful slogan. Vocal special interest groups can easily pressure pliable politicians to enact obstructions to free trade. In most countries, these obstructions to free trade have become very sophisticated. Blunt instruments, such as embargoes and tariffs, are too transparent to stand up to scrutiny from the WTO or other regulatory bodies. Restrictions now take the form of health and safety concerns, technical regulations, professional qualifications, the 'national interest' and other such ambiguous phrases. Planning restrictions on superstores in Ireland is a classic example. Our politicians never considered the need for such controls until UK retailers started to move in here. Once this occurred, and local retailers started to complain, the government decided to implement certain planning laws. The government may just as well have announced a tax on shoppers, which is what they have done by limiting consumers access to more efficient retailers. Instead, we are treated to long complicated explanations about the importance of the city centres and the evils of suburban shopping. Such concerns are nearly impossible to disprove conclusively, which is why, of course, these tactics are used in the first place. Ireland is not the only country that has used such methods. European commerce is littered with such trade restrictions masquerading in various disguises. Ireland is, in fact, one of the most liberal governments when it comes to free trade.

MONEY AND BANKS

The history of money is almost as interesting as money itself. Money as we know it, came into existence because of surpluses, and the desire of humans to prosper. Prior to the existence of money, there was barter, which was never an effective method of exchange. Barter limited the ability of people to trade surpluses because you had to meet someone who had what you wanted, and vice versa. This is known as a coincidence of wants. If there was no coincidence of wants, there was no trade and everyone was condemned to try to provide everything for themselves and not specialise and exchange surpluses.

Money was an unique invention, because it provided a medium which allowed people to exchange goods and services. Once the medium was in fixed supply, not easily duplicated, physically light, divisible, and commonly acceptable, it would be an excellent method of exchange. The trick was getting a medium that matched all of these criteria. Early societies used everything from special stones, shells, gems, even women until the Romans popularised the use of gold.

Gold was popular because it was physically in short supply, and, therefore, it was difficult to duplicate. It was also, in itself, attractive and used for various adornments. Near fixed supply and near fixed demand led to a stable 'price'. Gold was also easily divisible into coins. The one weakness of course, was that it was not physically light but the other advantages vastly outweighed this.

People however, now faced another problem with such a readily negotiable form of money, theft. People eventually became so worried about holding lots of gold coins, that they searched for a secure place to store them. The most popular secure location became goldsmiths, who by the nature of their craft, had a lot of gold on hand and so had secure strong rooms. These goldsmiths accepted other peoples gold for storage, it was a profitable sideline to their normal business. It was common practice to issue written receipts to each person for the gold they stored for them so that they could claim it back quickly. It also saved the goldsmith getting involved in complicated bookkeeping procedures. You produced the receipt and you got the gold. If you lost it then that was your hard luck.

The next development in money occurred because of laziness. Let's say you wanted to buy a new carriage. You went to the goldsmith, cashed in your receipt, received your gold, and took it to the carriage seller and transacted your business. The carriage seller then probably took this gold back to the same goldsmith and gave it to him for safe keeping. Eventually people simply got confident enough in the goldsmith, and too lazy to drag gold around the city endlessly, so they just exchanged receipts with each other. Assuming they had a receipt for the exact amount, or a combination of various receipts for the exact amount. In other words, I handed you a note from my 'bank', or a banknote! Paper money was effectively born.

Things nevertheless evolved a step further, as they always do, and the goldsmiths gave up working with gold and became full-time bankers. They realised that with all the gold in their strong rooms, they could write notes and lend them out to businessmen who wanted loans to expand their businesses. They rightly assumed that not everyone would cash in all the notes at the same time, so they could safely issue an excess of notes. There was now more notes than gold to match it, but experience taught them the ratio of notes to gold they could create and still keep afloat. The bankers now paid people a fee to keep their gold in their strong rooms, i.e. interest. They charged a higher fee to lend the money out, and made their living on the difference between these two interest rates. In the intervening years between then and now, not much of this core formula has changed. Bankers still make a large part of their profit from the difference between what they pay to depositors and what they charge to lenders.

To return to history again, things took a bad turn sometimes, when the bankers got too clever for their own good. Some bankers became convinced that so many people trusted them and that they would never request the actual gold back. These bankers started to produce even more banknotes, in the full knowledge that they were not backed by gold, but in the equal confidence that most people would not cash them in. Most times it worked, and the extra money supply would oil the wheels of commerce, creating more trade and jobs. Other times it could go badly wrong, inflation would occur or the public would become worried about the security of the notes. Members of the public would then go to the bank and demand gold. This could escalate to panic and become a self-fulfilling prophecy as all the gold the bank had was drained paying people back. This was known as a 'run on the bank'. The banker could go bankrupt and the city could go into recession because free trade would become obstructed by the panic and confusion over banknotes.

To cut a long story short, eventually the governments stepped in and mandated that only the governments could issue notes. Private banks could take deposits of notes and lend out notes but they could not issue them. Confidence in most notes grew to such a degree, that the government eventually revoked the right to receive a fixed amount of gold back per note. This was known as the ending of the gold standard. Since then, one could argue that things have been better or worse, it depends on which country you live in. You are, however, still free to buy gold at the current rate of exchange, i.e. the price per ounce, and many countries still back their currency with gold; many, however, do not. Some currencies, such as the US dollar, have attained such a strong and respected status, that they can be used to back other currencies, in the same way as gold was used before. In other countries, things have not always worked out well with paper currency. This was because various governments could not resist just printing more money, it always was such an easy option. If you print endless amounts of money, it loses its 'exchange' value is not fixed. Once the supply of money increases abnormally, you get hyper inflation, as occurred in Germany in 1923. To give one example, a newspaper in Berlin cost less than one mark in 1920 but by 1923 it cost 200,000,000,000 marks. Now that is serious inflation! The supply of money can have a serious effect on prices, depending on the degree of over supply.

Today's banks have evolved in many ways, but essentially they are the same as hundreds of years ago. Most banknotes have attained the stature which gold had before, because they are fixed in supply, difficult to counterfeit, easily divisible and physically light. The banks take these notes in, and then lend out most of them, they keep cash funds of around 10 per cent to give to customers who want notes back. However, fewer people require large quantities of notes now. This has been given the wonderfully illustrative name of 'fractional reserve banking'. It might be worrying to know that if more than 10 per cent of people went to one bank for their money at one time, the money would not be available. Do not fear however, as most banks in developed countries work together with a central bank to ensure this should never happen. Still banks are extremely conscious of appearing stable, this is why they build hugely expensive and ornate bank premises, with marble floors and granite columns. They need to give the impression of being permanent and enduring, because the depositor must have enough confidence in them. It is an interesting paradox that people would only want their money from a bank if they think the bank did not have it, if they think they have it, they don't want it.

SPECULATION

Speculation and speculators get extraordinarily bad press, this is because most people misunderstand the term. Speculators are seen as devious people, who have large amounts of money and spend their time distorting markets. This is a complete misrepresentation. Speculation is the essence of efficient markets. We are all speculators, if you exist in the capitalist world, you are a speculator. Let's look at an example.

If, every day, you take a fixed route to work, no doubt you pass many petrol stations, all of whom charge approximately the same price per litre for petrol. You, along with many other motorists, have little interest in where you buy your petrol as it is a homogenous product. Yet assume that one of these stations unilaterally raised the price of petrol by 10 per cent. You would no doubt stop filling up there, as would everyone else except for a few extremely foolish, or extremely rich, people. Business at this station would drop to such a degree that, unless the owners lowered its prices, it would go out of business. The combined act of many motorists will have forced the price they charge back into line or forced the station out of business.

Let's take another example. Let's say you are driving home and see a sign advertising widgets for sale at £1.00 each, a mile down the road you see another advertisement from a business offering to buy widgets for £2.00 each. One of these prices must be incorrect, the person selling them has their price wrong, or the person buying them has their price wrong. However, you would not care which one it was, you probably would go back and fill you car up with widgets and drive them to the other premises and sell them. Let's say you made £100 a trip, are you going to stop? Of course you are not, you are going to drive back and forth because you are making risk free profit. Eventually, of course, one of the businesses is going to go bankrupt if they keep transacting with you. You will have forced the inefficient firm out of the market by your actions, but your actions were legal and proper, the market was disrupted, and you brought it to equilibrium. What we are describing here is unlikely to happen in reality, but it does sometimes happen on larger financial markets. If you multiply matters up by a couple of hundreds of millions, you will arrive at what financial speculators do. They look for disruptions in the market and correct them. They provide a service by keeping all those who participate in the markets efficient, as you do with the local petrol retailers.

COBWEB THEOREM

I am not referring to the type that spiders make but the economic variety. The cobweb theorem is a very interesting phenomenon that explains a number of the price fluctuations we see in our society.

Let us assume that, this year, the price of wheat is at an all-time high. I should confess initially that I know nothing whatsoever about wheat farming, it is just a good example. Assuming that all farmers are rational and want to better their bank accounts, they decide to plant wheat to capitalise on this high price. When it comes time to harvest the wheat, there is an over supply because too many farmers planted wheat. The price of wheat falls because of oversupply, and many farmers stop planting wheat because of their bad experience with it. So, you guessed it, next harvest time the price of wheat is back up again due to low supply. So this oscillation of the price can tilt back and forth. What is essential in this process is that there is less than perfect information available to all farmers on what other farmers are doing. There must also be a time lag between investment, planting in this case, and supply to the market.

This does not just only occur with commodities, but can also occur with many other goods and services. Office space in London was a good example of the cobweb effect. In the booming 1980s in London, office space was at a premium. Office rents in London were very high and were making excellent returns for their owners. Many individual entrepreneurs and builders bought land and starting building office space. Places such as the docklands were developed, but when they were finally finished and ready for occupation, they realised that demand had also been met by many other property developers. The price of office space collapsed and no one built for years. Supply had drowned out demand. In the case of London, the economy had also suffered a downturn which exacerbated the problem. Many people do not understand why suppliers do not get together to plan out supply so that they all make the maximum amount of profit. This is a good point to raise, but in most cases it does not work. Humans are competitive, and do not wish to communicate what they are doing because they wish to gain a competitive advantage. In other cases, even when they do plan out supply, it fails. The Organisation of Petroleum Exporting Countries, is a good example of this. No matter how long they spend carving up supply, someone is always cheating and putting more crude on the market. Finally, in many countries such planning of supply is illegal because it is monopolistic, the government prefers to allow prices to fluctuate.

Just in case you are curious as to why it is called the cobweb theorem, it is because if you track the contractions and expansions on an X-Y graph, it tends to look like a spider's cobweb.

2

The Business Cycle

The only cause of depression is prosperity.

Clemunt Juglar

Most things in life run in cycles, the tides, seasons, even life and death. It should not then be so surprising to find that such cycles have extended into business and economics. These cycles are one of the most studied aspects of economics as they impinge on many areas of our lives. Since the 18th century, when John Law first encountered these cycles, other noted economists, such as Smith, Ricardo, Schumpeter, Keynes, and Friedman, have agreed on their existence, even if they have disagreed about the precise technical details.

Business cycles, at their most basic, are the waves of prosperity and abundance followed by recession and shortage that oscillate through our economies. They are neither periodic nor easily predictable and tend only to be easily defined and measured in hindsight. The amplitude of the oscillations of the cycles depend on many factors. Some of these oscillations are tremendous peaks and valleys, such as the roaring 1920s to the massive depression of the 1930s. Other cycles are more like rolling foot hills, and are hardly noticeable.

The important questions about business cycles are:
- What are the distinct phases of the business cycle?
- What controls their amplitude?
- What relevance do they have to Ireland?

In order to answer these questions I will 'build' a small economic model and run it through an almost complete business cycle.

Let us assume that there is a small village with less than 1,000 inhabitants. There are 200 people unemployed and the rest are productively employed in a cross-section of the various trades and professions. The local bank, for whatever reason, decides to lend out more money. A few citizens decide to take advantage of this and borrow money. They employ five previously unemployed people to build extensions on their houses. The five new workers need to buy lumber, glass and cement from the local merchant. This further increases the flow of business in the economy as a few more people are hired to supply the excess demand. A local merchant decides that business is going good and will do even better if things keep going like this. He decides to get ahead of the curve by expanding his store to include a little restaurant. He borrows money from the bank to do this. He too now needs more employees to build and staff this restaurant. Slowly as the unemployed workers are absorbed in various ventures, they now have wages which they can spend. Every extra pound earned, is a pound to be spent, and every pound spent is earned by someone else in this self-sufficient economy.

Soon the village is buzzing with near full employment. More people are feeling positive about their futures and borrow money in anticipation of earnings – something they would not have thought about before. They use this money to build a new house, or buy some luxury they had deprived themselves of for a long time. Each new purchase is produced in the village and so production increases even more. Practically everyone is now working, and some are even working two shifts just to supply what is demanded. Everyone in the village is optimistic and feels a major turn in the economy of the village has occurred.

The four master builders in the village are worked to capacity and have more work than they can deal with. Some people have even offered them extra payment to get to the top of the queue, so naturally they take these incentives. They are, after all, operating in their own self-interest. Soon this is starting to happen everywhere. The demand for some goods exceeds the amount produced, so the owner raises the price until the people demanding it equals what he has. A few factories have ordered extra equipment and are expanding to meet the new demand but it will be a few months before they come on-line.

The local banker has recently noticed that a few people have been spending too much. He calls them in to discuss their overdrafts and tells them to get their accounts back in order. The sharp talk brings these people to their senses and they realise that they have been overspending. Their anticipation of the good times was slightly ahead of reality, so they decide to engage in some retrenchment for a few months. They cancel orders they had made for a few items, and generally cut back on spending.

This small fall in their income affects a local merchant slightly and he realises that he has one too many people behind the counter. The owner lets one employee go. The newly unemployed worker tells a few people about her misfortune and they decide that they too may lose their jobs, and do some of their own retrenchment. Less money spent by these people, means less demand for goods, a few more people lose their jobs.

In the middle of this, the bank suddenly raises interest rates, and all the people who owe money now have larger repayments and a little less disposable income. Everybody with a loan has to prune spending a little. A large number of little spending cuts leads to a significant reduction in demand. A reduction in demand leads to a reduction in the number of jobs, the more jobs that go, the less money there is in circulation.

Suddenly merchants begin to realise that they have too much stock on their shelves, and cease ordering for a month to let supplies dwindle. The factories that had expanded now have too much capacity, large debts with mounting interest charges, and no firm orders. The rumour gets around that the factories are in trouble and people become nervous. The more nervous they are about their future, then the less they spend and the more they save for possible hard times ahead. They are, after all, operating in their own self-interest. One or two factories now go bankrupt due to low demand and high debts. There are now 200 people unemployed and people spend the bare minimum.

Provoked by this, the town council decide to act and instruct the bank to lend more money. The bank's response is that they have mounting bad debts and cannot risk much more money by making new loans in such uncertain time. In fact, they tell the council that they are only going to lend to the most blue-chip businesses and individuals. There is now a recession in the village and a credit squeeze by the bank, which deepens and prolongs the recession.

This is a very simple example with some definite flaws in the plot, but it does serve to illustrate most of a business cycle with a large amplitude. The distance between the heights of the boom and the depths of the bust were quite large. It does not, however, always reach such levels. If for example, the bankers had stepped in half way during the 'boom' phase and started to control the credit being issued in some way, then they could have turned the boom down before it became too overheated. The down-cycle would not then have been as steep because people and business would not have become as over stretched as they did. It is very similar to a pendulum. The distance the pendulum swings to one side as measured from the centre line, is a function of the distance it was from the centre line at the other side, when it was released. The quotation at the top of this chapter has its origins in this concept. Juglar, a famous Austrian economist was making the point that it was not through something going wrong that a recession occurred, but that something good went 'too right'. The ideal situation for all economists and politicians, is to avoid wild swings in the economy and to foster controllable stable growth in the country.

To return to our simple model, I want to break it up into phases. It is extremely helpful in understanding the whole process of a business cycle to look at its smaller segments.

1.   A small rise in employment levels.

2.   Expansion in the availability and 'cost' of credit.

3.   Expansion in the take up of credit, resulting in increased expenditure.

4.   An increase in the positive feedback mechanisms that amplify growth. A positive feedback occurs when an increase in a variable causes that same variable to increase again, and so on.

5.   Vigorous competition amongst lenders to lend, and a reduction in the quality of this debt.

6.   Expansion by business to meet growth, and anticipated growth.

7.   Price rises in goods and services which are in limited supply.

8.   Speculative increases in the prices of investment goods, such as real estate and shares.

9.   Euphoric feeling by a huge number of consumers, leading to further borrowing and spending in the expectation of a the continuation of the boom.

10.   Pinnacle reached and an imperceptible turning occurring in fortunes. A few individuals realise the top has been reached and react.

11.   Unwinding as a reduction in spending leading to loss of jobs, leading to reduction of spending.

12.   Defaulting on loans leading to credit squeeze which further depresses the economy.

13.   Spiralling downwards from negative feedback mechanisms, as more and more cuts in spending lead to cuts in demand and jobs, which leads to further cuts in spending.

These points are in roughly the order in which they occur, some are 'chicken and egg' situations and so it makes it difficult to order them precisely. What is essential to realise, for the time being, is that they do occur, and the precise order is not very important at the moment. I will examine each point a little closer as it is an excellent way to fully understand the broader picture.

The rise in employment can occur for any reason and, in fact, the expansion in credit may occur prior to the employment. In reality, however, they are processes which are intertwined throughout most of the up-cycle, more secure jobs leads to more loans and so on. The types of credit that expand are mortgages, term loans, overdrafts, credit cards, store cards, car finance, etc. The more money that is available, the more there is to spend. Each pound spent creates a pound of demand that reverberates throughout the economy. A famous Irish banker named Cantillion said, "Money had to change hands; otherwise it could not grease the wheels of commerce." Money circulates in an economy and the faster it circulates, the more active the economy becomes. Irwin Fisher, another famous economist, stated that: "Banks were the key to business cycles, as it was banks who created the money in the modern society."

Positive feedback mechanisms are a technical term for describing what some might call a feeding frenzy. Spending will create jobs, and jobs create spending. In a business cycle, the positive feedback mechanism is enhanced because of human psychology. Humans are not only reactive, but we also attempt to anticipate. If we anticipate good times, then we will spend confidently, if we anticipate bad times then we will slowdown our spending and save. These very acts do, of course, exacerbate both situations. Another positive feedback mechanism is whereby prices rise because the prices are rising. The more people buy a limited commodity, the further the price goes up. This rise in price attracts more buyers, and more buyers create further rises in price, etc.

If the 'price' of credit, i.e. interest rates, is lowered, then more people will demand credit. If you combine this with an overall increase in the demand for credit due to a general rise in employment, then all financial institutions will clamour to supply it. These institutions too, will be possessed with a mild irrationality as they are made up of many people who are very optimistic about the economy and will wish to capitalise on this optimism. The competition to lend more, and the general act of more money being lent, will lead to a reduction in the quality of that debt. The creditworthiness of the borrower will be slightly less than the banks would have demanded in leaner times. In some cases, the borrower may be an extremely bad credit risk, but the work overload, and desire to lend more money, may lead to this fact being overlooked.

With more money in the economy, there will be more demand. If the demand cannot be met, then prices will rise. If the village carpenter can only make ten new tables a day, and the demand is for fifteen, then the price will rise so as to ensure the demand and supply meet. In reality, this may not happen in one sudden move, but it will occur eventually. The important point to remember about a society is that each of its members is acting in his own self-interest. Adam Smith, yet another famous economist, Scottish this time, described it very well when he said, "The desire of bettering our condition comes from us in the womb, and never leaves us till we go to the grave." He further stated that these many individual and "selfish" actions led to outcomes, good and bad, that we did not intend: "He intends only his own gain, and he is in this, as in many other cases, led by an invisible hand to promote an end which is not part of his intention."

The above rise in prices has a name of course, inflation. Inflation can occur when too much demand is chasing too little supply. If supply can react to price changes, then prices may not rise, but in many cases, supply is fixed and it is impossible to react quickly to such changes.

Price rises in assets, such as real estate, also occur during many up-cycles. Many investors find that they can make a better return than keeping money in the bank, because of the lower rate on offer. Furthermore, it may seem shrewd to borrow money from financial institutions with which to buy assets. If you can borrow money at 3 per cent and buy property and get a return of 8 per cent, then many will do so. As investors increase demand for these assets, the prices will rise until the return from the investment is only above the 3 per cent by a sufficient amount to still make it worthwhile.

The euphoria felt by many consumers verges on the irrational. As the good times role, many assume that some big change or historic shift has occurred and things are going to go on growing in the same way forever. This has been an extremely common feeling in many up-cycles throughout the centuries. Many commentators during these periods have, of course, used historical reference to try to point this out, but the majority drown them out. It is a strong mixture of most consumers wanting to believe in something, and also believing that the majority of people could not be wrong. One of the most prominent economists of this century, John Kenneth Galbraith, said that the up-cycles always end in a wide case of temporary insanity.

The turning point is always reached, it is impossible to predict when it will be, or what will cause it. Sometimes it is a small event that cascades, sometimes a large one that lands with a thud. The net effect however, is that perceptions change and with them goes the mood of the people. The spending stops out of fear or unemployment, and events begin to unwind. It is a near mirror image of the matters on the way up. Spending falls, demand declines, jobs disappear and more spending cuts ad infinitum. This occurs over a long period of time of course, many months or years.

Someone once said that bankers are people who give you umbrellas when it is sunny and ask for them back when it starts raining. When the downturn gets going, some loans begin to turn bad, banks begin to realise that they were slightly over eager in their lending, so they begin to cut back. Financial institutions always tend to overcompensate and cut back on credit too much, in order to offset for their excesses in the boom. This of course, makes things even worse, but again everyone, including banks, is operating in their own self-interest. The bank manager who gave out too many loans, which are turning bad or doubtful, does not want to get into further hot water and so issues a memo that all loans are to be scrutinised even more carefully. The manager will also call in what credit he can to shore up the banks position. This is what is known as a credit squeeze.

Negative feedback mechanisms now set in, and retractions cause further retractions in the economy. Cuts in spending lead to cuts in demand, which affects employment and so, in turn, spending falls again. It is very difficult to stop this tide, because the more worried people become, the more they stop spending. It is nearly impossible for governments to alter the public's negative perceptions, in fact the more the government tries to calm the populace, then the more worried and cautious consumers become. The thinking goes along the lines of: "If the government is worried, then we should be even more worried."

The example we used at the start of the chapter, does not, of course, end at any one point. The recession will endure for a length of time, accompanied by pessimism on the behalf of consumers that will be the equal of the optimism they felt during the up-cycle. The pessimism and frugality will become a self-fulfilling prophecy, the less they spend, the worse it gets. The thaw will, however, come eventually as perceptions will again change. Prices will become so low that in due time, some astute entrepreneur will move in and buy. Slowly this spark will cause the economy to catch light, and demand will creep up, and off things go again.

The above example and discussion was fairly elementary, but it does give you an idea of a business cycle with a fairly large amplitude that was allowed to get out of control. This is not the normal situation, the amplitude of the cycle can be quite small as well.

There are many complicating factors that affect business cycles, it is, however, sufficient to repeat what I said at the beginning of this chapter: business cycles are not easily predicted, and can occur over very long periods, quite often they are only visible in hindsight. In the case where the up-cycle is extremely strong, it is usually fairly obvious to independent analysts what is occurring before the down-cycle begins. The question to look at next is: What distorts business cycles from a low undulating cycle to one of sharp rises and falls?

It is time we introduced one of the most important factors in the equation: the government. The government plays a vital role in the economy as it is the government's main function to control the economy. The village example was a closed unit with 1,000 citizens, dealing with an open economy and millions of citizens is vastly more complex. The government also has tools with which to attempt to control the economy, which I did not really introduce in the simple example. These tools can be divided into two main groups: monetary policy and fiscal policy. Monetary policy is basically the government policy on how it handle its own currency. This includes the quantity of money circulating in the economy, what interest rate to set, and what exchange rate policy to pursue, to name a few areas. Fiscal policy is the government financial policy, how to raise tax revenues and how to spend them. The fiscal policy is produced annually and is called a budget, whereas the monetary policy tends not to receive such focused attention.

It is, nevertheless, the monetary policy that we are more interested in at the moment. Governments usually have central banks that act independently, and attempt to steer the economy and control any excessive booms and busts, with the various monetary tools available to it. The most effective of these is the raising or lowering of interest rates. A central bank is a large financial institution that is 'owned' by the government and which acts as a banker for all the commercial banks. It also has the power to regulate many aspects of how banking and finance is conducted within the country. Ideally a central bank, even though it is a branch of the government, should be independent from the government of the day. Politicians quite often do not want to do that which is best for the country, but that which is best for their own election prospects.

Central banks have a tough job at the best of times. Trying to control a country is like trying to steer an oil tanker, it takes a long time to respond to any commands, and sometimes you tend to oversteer. The central bank has many data gathering mechanisms, which attempt to ascertain how the economy is performing. It watches these indicators very closely, hoping that, from experience, it can anticipate any significant moves in the economy. It is quite possible for an economy to grow steadily for a long number of years, if it is managed correctly by an experienced central bank. It requires close and prudent management to achieve this harmonic state. Central bankers are forever on the lookout for signs of a recession, or a boom, each are equally disliked by prudent bankers. The most prominent tool they use to control these movements away from stable growth, is interest rates.

If a central bank believes that the economy is heating up too much, it raises interest rates. A rise in interest rates makes borrowing more expensive. More expensive mortgages and other such consumer loans, absorb money from the consumer. The less money, then the less demand, and this puts the brakes on the economy. This is not a very popular action as you can imagine, but a little control in the short-term, ensures long-term prosperity. The current head of the American central bank,[2] Alan Greenspan, said, "The function of a central banker is to take the punch bowl away just as the party is getting going." Central bankers are always seen as spoiling the party, but they do so for a reason, they know that the economic 'hangover' is not worth the intoxication. The act of raising interest rates can also dampen the economy by making saving more attractive due to higher interest rates, and it also discourages businesses from borrowing for expansions because loans are more expensive.

Central banks also use interest rates to attempt to pull economies out of any recession they may be in. They cut interest rates in the hope that it will stimulate an economy by encouraging more spending. The consumers should have more money because mortgage repayments will have been reduced, borrowing will be more attractive, and saving equally less attractive. Basically the opposite of when they are attempting to slow an economy down. The aim of all central bankers is stable growth in an economy, not wild lurches in either direction.

I have finished this chapter on the function of central banks as it is at this point that the book shifts from theoretical examples into practice. Ireland, for the purpose of European monetary union, has to adopt the euro as its currency. The euro is not exclusively our currency, it is the currency of a group of much larger countries which we have chosen to use. This act means that our central bank, becomes a sub-branch of the European Central Bank (ECB). Ireland no longer has a central bank and, for all intents and purposes, we did not have one in 1998. This has deprived our government of the ability to shape monetary policy (interest rates) for Ireland's economic situation. The interest rate policy that is being pursued by the ECB and, in turn, our central bank, has little to do with economic conditions in Ireland.

---

2.   The USA does not have a central bank per se, but its Federal Reserve acts in the same capacity.

3

The Wrong Rate

*We are ever deceiving ourselves. But deep down
below the surface of the average conscience a still,
small voice says to us, 'Something is out of tune.'*

Carl Jung

The interest rate policy, which the Central Bank implemented in Ireland over the last eighteen months, is a case of the wrong interest rate, in the wrong place, at the wrong time. The reduction in interest rates has been the complete opposite of what we actually needed. Our Central Bank would have been better off if they had been obliged to pick the rate randomly. This is not a joke. If the Irish Central Bank had put the numbers 3 per cent to 8 per cent into a hat, and picked one, we would at least have had some chance of getting the higher rate we so desperately needed. Instead our rates were forced down against basic financial common sense which dictated they should rise. It is as if whiskey was given to a drunk man instead of black coffee.

The low rates we are being forced to use now are, in effect, somebody else's interest rate. Nobody could, or is, claiming that the rate Ireland is using is the correct one. The rate we are using has been chosen by the European Central Bank (ECB), and is designed for economic conditions that have nothing whatsoever to do with Ireland, we might as well be using the Spanish weather forecast to decide what to wear tomorrow. No analogy can indicate the irrationality of the rates that were forced upon our economy. The interest rate policy we are using is for countries, such as Germany and France, who have been in a mild to medium recession, and on a more basic level, have differently structured economies to Ireland.

The questions I will address in this chapter are:

- What are the effects of using the wrong interest rate?

- Why do we have to use this rate?

We need only look back to the example in the previous chapter, and hundreds of years of central banking wisdom, to see that the lowering of interest rates, in the face of strong economic growth, will lead to an powerful distortion of a normal low amplitude business cycle.

A lowering of interest rates is the main tool, which governments use to try to revive an economy which is in recession. Lower rates encourage borrowing, discourage saving and encourage rapid business expansion. Money floods into the economy and creates more demand and triggers a positive feedback mechanism creating even more demand. In times of recession, this might have been necessary, but we were not in a recession. We had already produced strong growth. The Irish economy improved rapidly during 1995 and 1996; this was the start of our up-cycle. We worked long and hard to pull our country out of a long, deep recession and economic misfortune, some would say mismanagement. The economy took off and jobs flowed in from around the world, especially the US and Asia. What was necessary in the face of this, was for the Central Bank to step in and raise interest rates to cool things down. We could still have kept the economy growing at a steady rate of 3-5 per cent, and we would have avoided the lurching growth that was provoked by a reductions in rates. Yet the Central Bank could not reduce rates, and the result is the chaotic prosperity we have now, and the inevitable down-cycle that will follow. I will discuss these topics in later chapters, but for now it is important to understand why the Central Bank could not step in and raise rates, as every other Central Bank would have done. The reason, and the only reason, was because Ireland had signed the Maastricht Treaty and so we were committed to joining European monetary union (EMU). It was this one obligation made many years ago that has come to haunt the Irish economy.

It is necessary, at this stage, to give a grounding in European monetary policy over the last twenty years and explain the reasons why the European Union moved towards a single currency.

European monetary union refers to the creation of a single currency throughout most of Europe, a union of money. This currency will be called the euro, and it is planned to be introduced between 1999 and 2002. The European Union, and before this, the European Community, has for a long time desired to eliminate the exchange rate fluctuations within Europe. The advantage of a single currency, as opposed to various fluctuating currencies have been put forward as:

- different currencies, which are constantly fluctuating, act as a barrier to trade;
- fluctuating currencies impose exchange and transaction costs on companies which trade across Europe;
- a single currency would be a strong catalyst to creating a single market in Europe. A single market means that many smaller national markets merge to create one larger market, which can benefit from economies of scale and specialisation;
- many different currencies appear to create many different prices. This can cause confusion when businesses attempt to compare prices across Europe.

It was for these reasons that the journey towards a single currency was embarked upon in 1979,[1] with the European monetary system (EMS). The main component of EMS was the Exchange Rate Mechanism (ERM). The ERM was supposed to limit the fluctuations between currencies by fixing bands within which they could fluctuate. Governments were obliged to intervene into the markets to maintain currencies within these bands.

This system looked good on paper, and it was also very easy to argue that it would work well, because it was in Europe's self-interest. However, it did not work very well, constant adjustments had to be made to the system. Essentially, the problem was that the people who designed this system forgot one important fact. No matter how much they used the word European, the European Union was, and still is, composed of many individual countries and each country is represented by national politicians.

The primal need of all politicians is to be elected, and elections are 'local' events, not European ones. As long as every national politician is elected locally, he or she will pander to his constituents, and it is unrealistic to expect otherwise. Throughout the 1980s, the ERM needed constant nurturing and doctoring. Numerous changes were made to the core rates in the ERM, the system was really just moving with the markets and not controlling them. In 1992-1993 the ERM effectively collapsed due to

---

1.   There were earlier moves, but I shall start here for brevity.

speculative 'attacks'. The final solution was to widen the bands
to such a degree that they accommodated most market fluctuations. This, of course, completely undermined the reasons for
which the ERM was set up in the first place. When I used the
word 'attacks' above, I put it in inverted commas because, as we
have seen from an earlier chapter, speculators do not attack,
they merely equalise. The use of the word 'attacks', gives governments and the designers of the ERM some face-saving mechanism. It gives the impression that the system was somehow crept
up upon and mugged. Speculators do not attack, no more than
a leak in your car would be caused by rain attacking your car.
Speculators simply expose the flaws in badly constructed systems.

One speculator, George Soros, even took the unheard of move
of warning the various EMS components prior to his 'attacks',
and gave them the opportunity to rectify it. No one listened, so
he walked away with over a billion dollars in profit, that is taxpayers money given to him by obstinate governments who were
deluding themselves. An essential problem with governmental
organisations, as opposed to people like Mr Soros, is that the
latter knows when he has made a mistake. Mr Soros has quite
frequently had his fingers burnt in the markets, but he cuts his
losses and walks away before those losses cripple him. Many
governments cannot do this, pride and the fact that they are
playing with other people's money, keeps them in the game too
long in the vain hope their luck will turn. Meanwhile, the ERM
was picked up, dusted down, and put back into service as a
precursor to EMU. All that the ERM was meant to achieve, we
are now told, EMU will achieve – and maybe it will.

Ireland had mixed experiences with the ERM. When we joined
in 1979, the UK did not join, and this led to the historic break
with sterling. The UK government at the time was never too
keen on 'Europe' and Mrs Thatcher did not much like the idea of
the ERM or a common currency. She felt that a single currency
controlled from 'Europe' would act against the better interests
of the UK. When sterling was eventually enticed into joining the
ERM, it proved a disaster, culminating in its ignoble forced with-
drawal in 1992 when it could not keep sterling within its bands.
It was this event that was the precursor to the broader failure of
the ERM. Anyone who questions why the UK is extremely nervous
of EMU now, need only look back to 1992 to see why. The UK
paid an extremely high price for its dalliances with European

monetary politics, and it is now very shy. This shyness is now overshadowed, but in no way reduced, by the desire of Tony Blair and Gordon Brown (the UK Chancellor of the Exchequer), to appear pro-European for political reasons.

The problems within the ERM did not stop the Maastricht Treaty from including a move towards total monetary union and a single currency. The Maastricht Treaty was actually composed before the ERM encountered serious problems. While the ERM was originally called the "glide path towards a single currency", the ERM was now considered not radical enough, and total European monetary union was required in order to energise a single European market. The Maastricht Treaty required that any country wishing to join monetary union, had to meet certain financial criteria to ensure harmony between economies. A fixed timetable was also laid out that dictated that the common currency would be introduced on 1 January 1999 as a separate legal currency, and that between 1 January 2002 and 1 July 2002,[2] it would be introduced in physical note and coin form throughout those countries that had chosen to join.

The framework for EMU, as written in the Maastricht Treaty, clearly stated that any country in the EU that wished, could apply for membership. However, if you read between the lines, it was inferred that only the more 'responsible' countries, such as Germany, Holland, and France, would initially form EMU. These countries were, in effect, moving in some form of harmony already, and their currencies tracked the Deutschmark so it was somewhat reasonable for them to form a single currency together. It was further envisaged, if not stated publicly, that the 'lesser' countries, such as Italy, Spain, Greece, and Portugal, would recognise the strong advantages of such a single currency block and reform their economies and join. The new European currency was planned to be a hybrid of the Deutschmark. This original concept was reasonably well-founded, because it was founded in reality and practicality. A small five or six country EMU, expanding slowly to take in less stable currencies, is a manageable proposition. Things however, did not work out this way.

In between the signing of the Maastricht Treaty and 1998, a recession hit Germany and France. It also became obvious that many countries in the EU took joining the common currency as

---

2.   Certain countries are attempting to reduce this time period.

a sign of national pride rather than economic sense. Italy, one of the least likely candidates initially, elevated the desire to join EMU to an almost national obsession. While Italy and others, made many positive, even dramatic, changes in their economies, they had, in my opinion, still not reached the calibre necessary to combine with the likes of Holland and Germany, to form a single currency. Yet in 1998, every single country who applied for entry into EMU, was approved. This occurred for a combination of reasons: the desire of Helmut Kohl to put his mark on Europe before the end of his political career, political compromises and mild political blackmail are but a few. Yet these currencies had still to meet a set of criteria, didn't they?

Yes they did, but it had, in effect, been agreed in a backroom deal prior to this that each country would enter. So it was just a case of squeezing into the dress for the prom and public show. Almost every single government which gained entry into the single currency, did so by massaging their budget figures to comply with the criteria that were laid out in the Maastricht Treaty.

The Maastricht Treaty had required that each country meet certain criteria on a sustainable basis, however, this was all but abandoned. To take one of the requirements as an example, the budget deficit. This was the most difficult criteria, as budget deficits had to be less than 3 per cent of gross domestic product, for the 1997 budget. It was already obvious that most EMU candidates would not meet this, and the antics that countries employed to reach this figure, became farcical.

- Italy had a euro tax which it levied in 1997 to reduce its deficit, but it plans to refund the money in 1999.

- The French government sold off part of its telephone company, and included these in its 1997 figures that were supposed to be sustainable figures that it could meet each year.

- The Germans, too, became desperate, Helmut Kohl even tried to revalue the gold reserves in the Bundesbank to create notional revenue to transfer to 1997 revenue.

It all became ridiculous, reminiscent of a once-off financial limbo dancing session, rather than sustainable convergence. In normal political circumstances, opposition parties would have screamed blue murder, but in the case of EMU, circumstances were different. Opposition and support for the European currency cut across the socio-economic divides which usually mark the line between competing political parties. The UK Conservative Party had torn itself apart fighting over EMU, and other European parties did not wish to follow its example. The outcome of this was that everyone looked the other way. Furthermore, on a supra-national basis, most governments were guilty, so no single government could point a finger, hence not one did.

Ireland was one of the few countries which almost met every criteria as laid out in the Maastricht Treaty, and this is terribly ironic, as the arguments for us being involved in the euro in the first place are weak. However, this is something we will discuss later. What is important now, is that a commitment to form a single currency was formally made by eleven governments in 1998, and this required a number of actions to be taken.

A currency is an important tool for a country. When a government has its own currency, it can set its own interest rates, exchange rate policies, and if necessary exchange control regulations. This allows it to adjust for economic conditions for that specific region. As we are going to introduce the euro, we are effectively going to be adopting another currency, and so we cannot control our interest rates or our exchange rates anymore. These will be controlled by the European Central Bank, the European version of our own Central Bank. Just as our Central Bank managed the punt, now the ECB will manage the euro from its headquarters in Frankfurt. It will decide the best interest rate policy for Europe as a whole. You cannot have a common currency and different interest rates. Can you imagine what would happen if a bank in Waterford was lending money out at 3 per cent and a bank in Dublin was giving 6 per cent on a deposit account. Immediately speculators would borrow vast amounts of money in Waterford and lodge them in Dublin and make a risk free 3 per cent. Eventually the rates would have to be harmonised between the two banks or one would go bankrupt.

Such is the case with the euro. If we are using the same currency as people in Germany and France, and their banks are lending money out at 3 per cent, then Irish banks could not offer 6 per cent on deposits. In dealing rooms around Europe, hundreds of millions of pounds can be moved in seconds, and the day the euro came into existence, Irish banks would be flooded with money to capitalise on a risk free profit.

Because of this, it was necessary for a euro-zone interest rate to be set and adopted by all countries joining EMU. Since we are so small and represent only about 1 per cent of the euro-zone population, we obviously had little weight in the decision. The interest rate that was chosen was effectively the German interest rate and everybody had to reset their rates to this level. For many European countries, this was not much bother as they were so close to it anyway, but for Ireland it was a serious event. It is here that things began to go wrong.

While EMU has promised prosperity and more for all, we were actually doing very well our own. Without EMU, we had managed to become a strong vibrant economy. We had arrived at a crossroads in history carrying all the right tools. We were members of the European Union, yet we carried little of the bureaucratic red tape with which many European countries are plagued. We had a young, energetic, well-educated workforce, spoke English and were politically stable. Foreign companies, especially American companies, saw an excellent European base. There was an ample supply of well-educated workers and these companies could have a base inside 'fortress Europe'. The economic boom in the US spread to our shores and matters were proceeding very well. We were on track to become the Hong Kong or Taiwan of Europe, small but significant.

It was at this point that our strong economic growth, and our entry into EMU, met face to face. In order to take the edge off our now booming economy and slow things down, the government needed to put interest rates up around early 1998, or probably earlier. As discussed previously, a rise in interest rates is necessary to control the business cycle. On the other hand, if we were to enter EMU, we had to start lowering rates to coincide with euro rates by 1 January 1999. The latter was, in fact, a contractual necessity, we had signed the Maastricht Treaty and had been accepted for entry to EMU. Our government was thus forced to start pushing rates down. Our Central Bank, which had to implement this policy, realised the dilemma and held out as long as it could, waiting until towards the end of last year before making the final cuts. It was trying their best to keep some control on the economy. But it was were bluffing with their cards facing the other players, everyone knew rates were coming down and the consumer behaviour reacted, even before the rates were finally cut to European levels. It is not, of course, the actual low rate that is the problem, it is the act of lowering the rate that seriously alters people's behaviour.

The main reasons why this policy persisted, even though the Central Bank knew it was wrong, was that:

- there is nothing we can do about it, EMU is a contractual obligation;

- consumers benefit in the short-term, and hence do not complain;

- the politicians are busy basking in the reflected glory, and making the best out of a bad situation;

- the Irish media finds it very difficult to swim against the tide of the first three points.

There is really nothing we can do about it. We signed a contract to join EMU and it is legally binding. There is, in fact, no mechanism to allow us to withdraw from EMU and regain sovereign control of our monetary policy. In either case, it would be too late, the damage is already done, it is now just a question of when, not if, the recession occurs, and how deep it is going to be.

The vast majority of consumers are enjoying the party and so there are no complaints. This is obviously the most difficult aspect of such distorted growth, it is almost impossible to convince people that anything is really wrong. The politicians are basking in the glory and claiming credit left, right and centre. I think it is a Persian proverb that states: "Success has a thousand fathers, and failure is a bastard child." The party may be wild but, unfortunately, it must end with the associated hangover.

While some in the media attempt to raise red flags, many others have been caught up in the euphoria, and jump on the bandwagon. I have seem so many headlines in Irish papers that repeat the same story, the boom is to continue forever, house prices will go on rising, there are thousands of more jobs coming. The mantra of the 'Celtic Tiger' is being repetitively chanted throughout the entire island. The 'experts' (usually auctioneers and/or stockbrokers) that frequently appear in the media, have given the final seal of approval. I have had so many people tell me that 'experts' have said that the boom is going to go on for ten years or more, so what am I worried about? Yet, nobody asks the vital question, who is it that pays the salaries of the 'experts'? Many of the 'experts' are employed by people who have a vested interest in advocating one side of the success story, and do not mention that caution might be prudent. This is not to imply any dishonesty on behalf of these people, but it must be realised that they, the 'experts' so often seen, are paid advocates. People have to ask two questions of an 'expert', what is your opinion on XYZ and who is currently employing you to stand here. It should not be surprising that someone, who makes commission on the sale of houses, is going to tell you that house prices are going to continue increasing. Or that someone who sells stocks is going to do the same thing. It is in their interest to keep the pot boiling and push one side of the story, and they should not be faulted for this. They are, after all, operating in their own self-interest, as we all do.

While I have discussed much here, I have proved very little of it, and the rest of the book will hopefully do this. I start with a discussion of the physical signs of overexpansion in the economy and move on to the actions of consumers, the credit boom, the house price bubble and the many other aspects of the Irish economy that support and buttress my arguments.

4

Straining At The Seams

Abundance, like want, ruins many.

Eastern European Proverb

Growth in an economy is like speed, it can be good and it can be bad. 550 mph is a reasonable speed for a 747 that is five miles off the ground. On the other hand, driving a car at 40 mph past a school at lunch-time, could be reckless endangerment. The essential difference is control. Economic growth is much the same, there can be too much growth, as well as too little growth. It is my contention that the current business cycle in Ireland has become wildly distorted and the excessive growth in the economy has now become a risk to any growth at all. There are, however, those that can argue what is 'too much'. Maybe 4 per cent was too much ten years ago, but now 8 per cent or 10 per cent is realistic. There is a simple solution to ascertaining what a manageable rate of growth for an economy is: examine the effects of the current rate of growth and to determine how the economy is reacting to such growth. Excess growth has two prominent effects on an economy, the first is physical, the second is the effect of the psychology of consumers in that economy. In this chapter, I will examine the physical aspect of the growth rate experienced in Ireland, as it is reflected in the infrastructure. It is my contention, that the economy is straining at the seams and simply cannot deal with current growth rates. It takes time to expand an infrastructure commensurate with the economic activity. If the infrastructure cannot grow as fast as the economy, then costs are going to be incurred by all those in that economy. These costs are incurred for three main reasons.

1.   Congestion of the infrastructure.

2.   The costs associated with attempting to expand the infrastructure rapidly to catch up with the economy.

3.   The costs of over-expansion in some areas because decisions
      made during the boom, are not measured or reasoned but
      just reactive.

Every boom has its epicentre, usually the capital city, and in
Ireland's case it is no different. Dublin is the furnace of this boom
and its fires are burning brightly. It is in Dublin, therefore, that
the clear signs, and costs of excessive and irrational growth are
obvious. The areas I will look at to illustrate this point are:
•   road transport;
•   Dublin airport;
•   taxis;
•   private infrastructure.

The greatest visible demonstration of a infrastructure groaning
under the rapid expansion, are the roads in and around Dublin. It
may be difficult to demonstrate the reckless monetary policy, but
the roads provide an excellent, and visible, metaphor. I first noticed a year ago that the roads had become clogged. Every two or
three months when I returned home, matters became incrementally worse until one day I realised the morning rush 'hour' had
almost merged with the lunch-time rush 'hour', which had merged with the evening rush 'hour'. And yet the problem still gets
more serious. New cars are flooding the streets at an incredible
rate. Between April 1997 and April 1998, 64,000 cars were reg-
istered, and I doubt this growth has slowed. Logic tells us, and
their driving demonstrates, that many of these new cars are first-
time drivers. The most prominent sign of prosperity in our society is a car. It is the first consumer commodity that people aspire
to when finances allow.
    Cars and their drivers create demand for road space in the same
way that shoppers created the demand for salmon. Yet you cannot run out and order more roads. You can rush to build more,
widen some, but in the short and medium-term, the supply of
road space is relatively fixed. In fact, in most built up areas of
Dublin, road space is fixed solid. The increase in demand and
limitation in supply, leads to a rise in the 'price' of roads. This is
not a direct monetary cost, but one of resources. The largest cost
of road use is paid in time, and time is finite, we all have 24
hours a day to spend. The more cars on the streets, the more
congestion there is, and the longer a journey takes. The final

cost, of course of a person's time, is money. On a very basic level the cost of more cars sitting in traffic, is a larger petrol bill and more pollution, but this is insignificant compared to the actual cost of the drivers' time. There are a number of ways that this cost is incurred.

1. A self-employed person engaged in a business or profession has less time to work if he is sitting in a traffic jam. He either suffers the loss, works longer hours, or raises what he charges per hour. This can also eventually tend to restrict such activities as doctors making house calls.

2. An employee of a company who has to be at his place of employment at a fixed time, must leave home earlier. The longer commute to work means he gets into work in less than peak condition. Furthermore, he will eventually seek compensation from his employer in higher wage demands for this extra time. There is also a social cost on families, but this is difficult to quantify, so I will leave it aside.

3. From an employer's view point, he either pays the extra wage demanded by employees, or he risks losing them to another firm which is more conveniently located. Either way, he has to pay higher wages or pay extra recruitment costs.

4. Businesses suffer other associated costs due to more difficult delivery conditions. More traffic congestion means higher delivery charges, and less certain delivery times. The longer a truck spends on the road, then the higher the costs associated with the goods it is delivering, and the more pollution and obstruction inflicted on the general public.

According to Mr Michael McDonnell, the chief executive of CIE, the cost of our traffic chaos is now £1.2 billion a year. This figure no doubt includes many 'costs' that are difficult to quantify, such as quality of life and deterring future investment. So let's cut the figure in half and say that the cost of congested roads are £600 million. That is around two-thirds of the 1998 budget surplus. This brings us nicely into the government's public transport policy, or should I say, the lack of one.

I would like to say that I see a transportation policy in Dublin, but I do not. Although I must confess I know very little about transportation policies, I simply base my judgement on what I see, and in trying to transport myself around Dublin: a frustration that I am sure most others feel a lot more than I do. It has become fashionable to compare Dublin to the cosmopolitan cities of the world, in fact, I read recently one commentator describing Dublin as the most cosmopolitan city in the world. While I love Dublin, and prefer it to any city in the world, in terms of public transportation Dublin is a backwater. We are the only capital city in the industrialised world, that has no purpose built modern transportation system. There are developing countries run by governments of questionable democratic credentials that have better transportation systems, and by inference I must assume transportation policies. I lived in Venezuela for over a year and Caracas had a clean and efficient underground, and this country is categorised as a developing country with a small fraction of our GDP per head. I lived in Vienna for an equal amount of time, and they had an underground system, a tram system and electrified autobuses. All working in harmony to deliver people around the city.

Before anyone points the DART out to me as a transportation system, the DART is an old rail line with new rolling stock on it. It was not purpose built, simply utilised. It serves the coast of Dublin, and is an excellent system for what it does, but it cannot be extended or expanded to serve the majority of the city. Granted that it was a great idea, it has worked well, but what Dublin needs is an underground system. Much has been made of the Luas light rail system, but where is it? All I see at the moment is consultations, committees and talk. Everyone is talking, but nobody is doing anything. Reality is about results, you cannot put passengers on 'talk'. The reality is reflected in the comments made by Mr McDonnell to the Joint Oireachtas Committee on Public Enterprise and Transport. He said that the government policy on transport is one of "schizophrenia" and that the bus system in Dublin, the only currently viable public transportation system, is being starved of funds. Such comments from the person who runs Dublin's only city-wide transportation system, should not be ignored. Meanwhile, the government is waving around its 1998 budget surplus. The surplus is coming, in part from creating the traffic chaos in the first place. If the buses were funded properly, then there might be no chaos, but, then again, there would be no surplus either. From someone who is looking in from the outside, I cannot understand how the government is willing to pay out vast sums of money to 'deaf' soldiers, but cannot fund Dublin Bus.

In a speech to an ICTU organised conference, Public Enterprise Minister, Ms Mary O'Rourke, spun the government's version. She inferred that it was Dublin Bus who was to blame because they could not make agreements with the unions to allow for expansion. She also said that the government did not intend to spend much more money on road construction, as this was not the solution. She also stated that economic growth had occurred more quickly than the Dublin Transport Initiative had anticipated, and this was the main cause of the problem. The short-term solution was to take money from the Luas project to buy a few new buses. From this statement, I think we can safely infer what mode of public transport we will be using in five years time. We shall all be on what few buses we have, while some government committee argues about whether the Luas should be turning left or right at O'Connell Street.

It is possible to draw a number of conclusions from the current transportation situation in Dublin.

1.   A transportation policy must be proactive not reactive. The government only began to decide on a new transportation system when it needed one. That is not policy planning, it is a knee-jerk reaction. Policy planning is obviously about planning. Planning means anticipating something and being prepared for it. It does not mean holding a committee meeting to think about buying a fire extinguisher when the fire is raging around you.

2.   Uncontrolled growth is straining the infrastructure of Dublin and costs hundreds of millions of pounds every year. That cost is, as always, passed on to the consumer eventually. It absorbs resources and produces nothing. It is a cost to the country, and the cost grows as more cars pour on to the streets.

3.   The solution to the problem unfortunately involves plunging the city into more chaos, which consumes even more resources in the short-term. This is the horns of the dilemma, in order to cure the patient, you have to kill him.

If growth had been controlled in Dublin to about 4-5 per cent per annum, the government would have had some small amount of breathing room in which to operate. Plans could have been

drawn up and construction started without the amount of traffic that is on the streets now. The kind of chaos witnessed on the
roads in Dublin, is directly linked to too much growth in the
economy, which is the result of our Central Bank's inability to
control our interest rates. More money buys more cars, and
'cheaper' money encourages more car loans.

If readers think I am being too negative or alarmist, they need
only look to the comments from the AA. The AA describes the
current traffic situation as a "disaster". With new cars coming on
to the streets everyday, the government not inclined to build new
roads, and Luas further away than Mongolia, then one can only
surmise which direction we are heading. Yet all is not lost, there
are solutions, in fact there are some very simple solutions that could
be implemented within weeks. They may not be popular, but they
would be effective.

At this stage there are only two main paths to alleviate the
crisis, and the most effective requires intrusive government of the
type that no one likes. However, we have no alternative and the
longer we wait the worse it will get. The two options are:

- do nothing and let the traffic chaos take its own toll to the
  point where the costs associated with driving are so high
  that some people simply stop driving; or

- the government takes decisive action and legally forces cars
  off the roads.

The latter is the best solution, as it can be implemented quickly.
The plan I would suggest, would be to alternately ban odd and
even numbered cars from the roads for one day (numbers being
the number in the registration plate). This should be enacted into
law for a period of two to three years. Weekends could be probably be excluded without too much difficulty. This would mean
on Monday, odd numbered cars could use the roads, on Tuesdays
even numbered cars could use the roads, etc. and at the same
time, provide more buses to absorb the extra traffic and enact
some system to facilitate car pooling. This time could be used to
build whatever transportation system is necessary to serve Dublin
effectively so as to entice people away from cars and then repeal
the ban. Even though this would be met with initial resistance, it
will achieve a number of things. It will free up the streets of Dublin
for public service vehicles and delivery vehicles, it will also allow
some breathing room for the necessary construction work to take

place. It would slow down car sales, and I think drivers would eventually become accustomed to it, and even like it. Better to drive hassle free in Dublin for one week out of two rather than the alternative, which is the city slowly strangling in traffic.

Yes, there are loopholes in the system, yes, there would be hardship cases, yes, rich people could buy second cars, but nothing is perfect, it is a radical solution to a problem that will not go away. We are, eventually, going to be forced into such a system, so we might as well get the pain over with now.

Dublin airport is another example of a piece of physical infrastructure that simply cannot deal with the excessive growth forced upon the city. Without the necessary time to expand in an orderly fashion, it too is drowning in excess capacity. Too much growth can be bad when you cannot deal with it appropriately.

Michael O'Leary, the head of Ryanair, described the airport on a busy morning as akin to "the black hole of Calcutta". I have recently arrived and departed from the airport on quite a number of occasions, and can confirm his diagnosis. Aer Rianta is struggling to expand, but they can only expand in 'Lego brick' fashion, which is no real solution. What is needed is probably a second terminal. It is extremely difficult to define the costs associated with the airport overcrowding. All I know is that every foreigner who passes thought Dublin airport and leaves with a bad impression, is negative PR for the country. Negative PR will cost us future tourist business, the excesses of today are paid for tomorrow.

Dublin airport is, of course, responding. Traffic estimates are now put at 20 million for 2005, but why should we believe this forecast when the forecast in 1990 for 1998 was so far out? Why should they be right now? Here we begin to encounter a derivative of the cobweb theorem in action. Dublin airport, when traffic was low, predicted too low a future figure and did not produce enough 'supply' of airport space. Now that demand for airport space is up strongly, their predictions may simply be extrapolation forward from this point. Predictions quite often tend to be a function of recent growth rates, and while this appears superficially logical, when you think about it, it cannot be a very informative method of forecasting – if it was this easy, business forecasting would be near perfect, and it isn't. It may happen that they have now overestimated this passenger figure and if they act on this to produce the commensurate amount of supply, then demand will have fallen and there will be an oversupply of airport space. Yes, Aer Rianta is caught in a dilemma, it does not have enough capacity to deal with current demand, and it will probably have too much in five years time if they expand based on forecasts done in the heat of the moment.

It is of course, not really the fault of Aer Rianta, as it only controls the airport, not the economy. The reduction in interest rates has led to uncontrolled growth and put more money in peoples pockets. Every single person I know in Dublin has been to the airport in the last six months to travel, a weekend in Manchester or New York, a quick holiday here, a business trip there. Five years ago, such 'luxuries' were, possibly, annual events. There is, of course, nothing wrong with such prosperity, rather the rate at which it has occurred. Airports cannot respond as rapidly as people do. Lurching growth upsets many balances.

In the private sector, there are also many concerns with dealing with the rapid expansion, and taxis are in particular an enigma to me. Again we are dealing with a situation where the number of taxis cannot expand to meet the supply. When I say cannot, I mean the system, as it is designed, cannot. It is the taxi drivers who, acting in their own self-interest, are blocking expansion. The government does not seem willing or capable to tackle the situation.

I do not know anyone, except taxi drivers, who think there are enough taxis in Dublin. I have stood at Dublin airport for an inordinate amount of time in queues of people waiting for taxis. In one such queue, I talked to an American businessman who could not believe it. He said he had been in at least twenty different cities in the last year and had never waited so much as five minutes for a taxi. The old supply and demand rule occurs again. If supply is fixed and demand increases, then the price rises. Even though taxis are metered, this does not matter because economics finds two ways around this. The price of a taxi becomes not only the money price, but the total resource cost of getting a taxi. The price you pay to the taxi driver must be added to the time you waited for the cab because of limited demand. The American businessman I met in the queue, waited about twenty minutes for a taxi. His time was going to be paid by someone, so we can add this on to the total cost of that taxi for the economy. The second way in which the price rises, is that the taxi driver just charges you a higher price. Even though prices are supposed to be metered, I was in two taxis recently, one from the airport, and the meter was not on, the fare was in my estimation £4 above what it should have been. Why didn't I report it to the carriage office? Well, like everyone else I was just too busy and could not be bothered. The taxi drivers apparently know more about supply and demand than our government does.

At the heart of the issue, is the system which controls the number of taxis in Dublin. The taxi plate system which limits the number of taxis on the streets, is an anachronism of simple-minded economics. The idea that you sell the right to people, with no qualification other than a driving licence, to be taxi drivers in our capital city is indefensible. Taxis are a public policy issue, especially in the current difficulties with traffic in Dublin. What encouragement does it offer anyone to leave the car at home and rely on private transport, when the chances of getting a taxi are near impossible at peak times.

We need only look to most other European capitals to see the various solutions to the taxi problems, rather than taxi drivers selling plates at inflated prices. Yes, I realise if the government dramatically increased the number of plates, then the price would fall, but so what. The vested interest of a small number of people, cannot outweigh the rights of a significant majority. The various options the government has are:

- to scrap the plate system and introduce an exam-based system, as in London. The exam known as 'the knowledge' requires that taxi drivers have intimate knowledge of every single street in London. If you visit London, you will quite often see prospective taxi drivers on scooters with maps on the handle bars driving endlessly around the streets preparing for the exam. Dublin is vastly smaller than London, such an exam could not be as difficult, and at least would result in a steady stream of qualified people coming on to the market;

- to introduce part-time licenses that allow drivers to operate at certain times and on certain days of the week. Weekend plates would definitely alleviate the Friday and Saturday night rush;

- if the government is not going to change the system, then at least benefit from it, by restricting the right to transfer plates, and auctioning ones that have not been used for a period of three months. This way, the exorbitant price of plates can be put into the government's coffers and not private hands.

The government, again, has its fingers in this transport issue and it has the power to address the problem with taxis. Yet it chooses to do nothing, but tinker with the system. Dublin needs taxis, so why do they not solve the problem? Probably because the government does not want to rock the boat. The traffic chaos becomes self-perpetuating because each pressure group knows that they can cause more chaos by protesting in Dublin at peak times. The government are too afraid to deal with the taxi drivers because of the protests that would result. However, the path of least resistance is rarely the best path.

The last element of infrastructure which I wish to discuss, is related to something that is exclusively in private hands, this is hotel rooms. The shortage and cost of hotel rooms in Dublin has created dual problems. Firstly, the price of a hotel room is extremely high. I pay less for a hotel room in New York than I do in Dublin, which seems strange. Yet, it is a case of supply and demand, and so be it. However, I get a feeling that hotel rooms are going to become to Dublin, what office space was to London.

Hotel rooms in fact, represent a classic cobweb situation. A shortage of hotel rooms in the last three years has led to a sudden sharp reaction from the private sector to supply hotel rooms. A big article in the *City Life* section of the *Irish Independent*, announced that, "40 new hotels for Dublin in just two years". This sounds like a wonderful announcement, and in many ways it is. It also, however, indicates that what is occurring is that various business interests who have limited contact with each other, are reacting to high prices; just the same as the farmers reacted to the high price of wheat in the example used in Chapter 1. Each is acting in what they see as their own best interest, and is hoping to produce a profitable business venture. It takes a couple of years for hotels to be financed, planned, built and opened. This time lag allowed more hotels to be planned and started.

The result will be an over-supply of hotel rooms when all the supply comes on-line, simply because each new participant entering the market did not have full information on who else was entering it. Neither did they have information on what the 'right' number of hotel rooms for Dublin was. To compound their problems, the economy will probably have turned down just as the last supply of rooms is hitting the market. Thus, demand will begin to fall away just when supply is peaking. In London during the late-1980s, a similar effect happened with office space. At one stage in the mid-1980s, office space was in short supply, so many intelligent astute investors rushed to build office space. However, none of them knew at the time they started the planning and building, who else was going to supply office space.

The result was a glut that lasted years, and there were places, such as the docklands, which were a ghost town. Investors like Paul Reichman, who was one of the shrewdest real estate investors of the time, ended up buried in debt. This occurred because when he made the decision to build huge office blocks, developers lacked complete knowledge about what other market participants were doing. If Mr Reichman, who was an experienced property developer, can make mistakes, then so can all the rest of us. The positive side of this will be that the price of hotel rooms will fall in Dublin when the excess supply kicks in, and demand falls away. There will, I predict, be some excellent bargains not only in hotel rooms in Dublin in 2000 and 2001, but in hotels as well. Every cloud has a silver lining.

I hope now, you are beginning to understand the problems that too much growth is bringing upon the economy of Ireland, and Dublin in particular. It is, of course, not an exaggeration to claim that Dublin itself has become a mini economy inside the economy of Ireland. Greater Dublin has become its own island, with unique set of concerns and problems. The real steam behind this up-phase in the business cycle, is the behaviour of consumers. It is consumers who inhabit the city of Dublin, not cars or buses. In the next chapter we move into the broad area of consumer psychology.

5

Consumer Psychology

I can calculate the motions of heavenly bodies,
but not the madness of people.

Isaac Newton

In the final analysis, economics is always about people. It is people who buy, and people who sell. It is people who make assumptions, and people who expect certain outcomes. Business cycle theory is as reliant on the mechanics of finance, as it is upon the activities of people. This chapter explores some basic theories of psychology that can affect all of us. I will move on to demonstrate how these theories are seen in practice in the more extreme business cycles. It is, however, important to separate the theory initially, to obtain a clearer understanding.

The three areas I wish to look at are:

- the herd instinct;

- group think;

- perceptions.

We all like to think we are individuals, and choose our path in life independently of everyone else, but, unfortunately, this is not always the case. Society dictates that we conform to many acceptable norms in order to make that self-same society function efficiently. We, ourselves, also wish to conform more that we think, the herd instinct is much stronger in us than we would like to admit. This herd instinct comes from an anthropological throwback to our instinctual desire to survive. In many nature documentaries, you will see herds of antelopes or wildebeests moving lockstep across the Serengeti as they are pursued by a cheetah or lion. The animals know that once they becomes separated from the herd, they will be lunch for the pursuing feline predator. There is safety in numbers. This instinctual desire to move with each other has left strong imprints on the minds of humans.

I once watched a documentary about a celebrated experiment conducted in an American university in the 1950s. It was one of the most fascinating studies I have seen, yet it was incredibly simple. A psychology professor advertised for volunteers in the campus newspaper. Each candidate selected was asked to fill out a questionnaire, which asked, amongst many others things, how independent or rebellious people thought they were.

Selected candidates were then individually brought in to a room and introduced to nine other students who were supposed to be part of the study. What the newly introduced candidate did not know, was that the nine other participants were 'in' on the experiment along with the professor. The assembled group of ten people were then told that they were going to be tested on their 'perception of length'. The professor then held up a large white cardboard display with two thick black lines, marked A and B. He asked students to indicate which line was the longest. Now it was obvious that line B was the longest, not by much, but still noticeably longer.

The students were then asked one by one to answer. The first student said A, so did second, the third and so on. A hidden camera was focused on the real 'white mouse' of the test, student number ten. His face became curious as the first student answered A, and even more curious as the second student answered A. It was obvious he was confident, and rightly so, that B was the longer line. One by one, each of the students answered A, when it got to him he nervously answered B. No one said a word, and the professor noted down the results, and moved on with a second display. Same story, two lines, one obviously longer than the other, and all nine students answering that the shorter one was the longest. By the time they reached the real subject of the experiment, his face was visibly contorted, he looked extremely worried as he gave the correct answer, but different to what the previous nine had answered. The process of disagreeing with the vast majority, no matter that he was correct, was extremely daunting. By the third display he gave in! He agreed with the other nine students that shortest line was the longest, he was visibly shaken. By the fourth, fifth and sixth display of lines, he was agreeing, no angst on his face, just resigned acceptance.

The professor went through many students, and every single student eventually gave in to the majority opinion no matter how it conflicted with what his own eyes were telling him. Each student eventually doubted their own ability to see which line was longest. The professor eventually isolated a group who described themselves on their questionnaires as 'strongly independent' and 'strongly rebellious' and one by one, each of those gave in to the majority decision. I think it took five or six rounds to break the most resilient, but every single student eventually gave in. It was fascinating to watch as the camera focused on the students mental struggle, before folding and going with the majority decision. From then on, it was automatic, each student just agreed without offering much resistance. We are all subject to such pressures if the circumstances are right, all of us think we are not, but, unfortunately, we are.

'Group think' is a phenomena that can occur when you have a highly cohesive group of people, a committee for example. Group think will occur when a group lets its desire to conform as a group affect its ability to make good decisions. The signs of group think are:

- **a perceived immunity to reality**: the group's members believe that success can be achieved no matter how overwhelming the circumstances are;

- **a strong offensive against any opponents**: opponents of the group are labelled as insipid, stupid or ignorant;

- **those who dissent are pressured to conform**: anyone inside the group who dissents is pressured to fall back into line by the rest of the group;

- **self-censorship by group members**: members of the group, who may disagree with its decisions, keep silent because they do not wish to rock the boat;

- **a misinterpretation of silence**: each member of the group believes that the silence of the other members is tacit approval and so assumes there is unanimous agreement on the issues;

- **consolidated justification**: the group itself believes it cannot fail, this is because members are blinded to any potential signs of trouble;

- **mind guards**: members of the group emerge to act as guardians of the groups norms. Information contrary to its position, and criticism of the group, is held back from the group.

Many significant historical blunders can be directly attributed to
group think. Quite often when interviewed individually later,
many members of a group state that they never concurred with
the decision of the group, and that they were even vehemently
opposed to it. But records will show that all voted for it, or appeared to agree with the position. When group think occurs, responsibility tends to be shifted to the group as a whole, if something goes wrong, the group or committee as an amorphous legal
entity, is blamed by the individual members of the group. You
arrive at a strange position – jointly liable, but individually inno-
cent. It would, of course, be wrong to say that all groups, or
even most groups, experience group think. Group think is something that occurs under certain circumstances when the cohe-
siveness of a group is extremely strong, usually under times of
stress or pressure.

The perceptions of individual consumers are critical to how
they behave financially, and the behaviour of consumers is critical to the economy. The economy is, after all, composed of millions of consumers. Basically we can state that a consumer who
perceives that his own financial future is secure, will spend more
money than one who perceives that his financial future is not secure. We can put this in to a simple formula:

spending = f (of consumers' perception of their prosperity).

Consumers' perception is based on a few factors, including how
he or she gathers, processes and interprets information. It would,
necessarily, include an element of experience and memory. However, if such experience is lacking, perceptions will more than likely
be based solely on the current information consumers receive
from outside sources, and how they process that information.

Let us look at some examples. Japanese consumers for the last
couple of years, have been spending very little because the country is in a quagmire. Many consumers have money but just do not
wish to spend it, in case they need it in the future. The government, in an attempt to stimulate the economy, has been lowering
interest rates to try to encourage people to take their money from
the banks and spend it. This, as we have seen, is fairly standard
government policy in the face of a recession. Yet the perception
of Japanese consumers is so entrenched, that even interest rates
of ½ per cent or 0 per cent cannot encourage them to remove
their money from the banks, stop saving, and generally increase

their spending. There is really nothing more the Japanese government can do with interest rates. They could, in theory, reduce rates to below zero, or into negative numbers, which would effectively penalise people for keeping money in the bank, every month the bank would deduct interest from your account. What would become even more surreal is that if you borrowed money, the bank would pay you interest every month! Now that is a mortgage I could live with.

Even with the rate of interest in Japan so low, it is not enough to stimulate growth, so the government has come up with a scheme of which I think most consumers around the world would approve. The Japanese government is proposing to give a large group of citizens about US$130 in vouchers to spend in shops and department stores. The hope that is that this spending will be the spark that ignites the economy. However, some commentators have suggested that consumers may simply sell the vouchers at a discount to others, or just use them to purchase items they would normally buy. In both cases, they would then put this extra cash in the bank. This is a demonstration of how the perceptions of consumers can become so ingrained in their minds, that not even 'free money' will encourage them to spend.

The reverse is equally true. Governments attempting to control their own populace from the excesses of spending, sometimes have to take money from them with higher interest rates, higher taxation or cuts in government spending. It is a terrible to think the government must take our money from us like children, for fear of what we would do with it, but such is the case. Unless individual consumers begin to feel financial pain, then their perception of their prosperity will not change.

The above three topics are essential components to a fuller understanding of the human side of the business cycle. It is relatively easy to demonstrate how all three of those topics are playing strong parts in the current up-phase of the business cycle in Ireland. The difficulty, for me, of demonstrating this, is that I am entering into the extremely sensitive area of the human psyche. Nobody wishes to be described as following the herd, we strive though our actions, our careers and even our dress, to individualise ourselves. Neither does anyone wish to believe that they have done something irrational. However, the function of this book is to demonstrate that the economy in Ireland is irrationally exuberant, and this necessitates pointing out the irrational activities that consumers are pursuing. The natural reaction may be to attack the messenger, I hope this is not the outcome in this case.

John Kenneth Galbraith, arguably the most eminent economist alive today, has experienced many up and down-cycles, he was even around to witness the great crash of 1929. Recently, on his 91st birthday, he gave an interview on CNN. He ruefully commented to the effect that all economic booms end in temporary insanity for a majority of the population. This is the case in Dublin.

The herd instinct, which so protects animals from predators, can, in financial matters, lead to ruin. The essential problem is that a large group of people can easily be deceived, and by a process of near perpetual motion, deceive others in turn. Financial crises throughout history have shown this to be so. If the up-cycle of a boom gets out of control, then people will extend themselves beyond their financial means, and not allow for any reasonable expectation of a downturn in the economy. Each set of consumers in every boom, always thinks their situation is unique and that a singular shift in fortunes is taking place, and this is the case in Dublin. Let us take an example from centuries ago to illustrate how similar sentiment is in every boom. This is a description of France in the early 1700s from Lars Tvede's book *Business Cycles.*

> *Although only four years had passed since France had been in the deepest despair, the entire country now started to virtually boil over in joy and happiness. Prices on any luxury items began rising and the production of rich laces, silks, broad-cloth and velvets increased many fold. Artisans' wages rose four fold, unemployment fell, and new houses were built everywhere...In Paris, the pot was boiling more than anywhere else. It was estimated that the population of the capital increased during this period by 305,000 inhabitants. Often the streets were so crowded with new carriages that nobody was able to move...soon a new word was added to the French vocabulary, 'millionaires'.*

Within a number of years, France was in recession again, the growth that inspired the boom suffered because the boom could not be controlled.

It is essential for readers to grasp that I am not questioning the grounds upon which our economy grew. There is always fundamental growth, the problem is that the growth was allowed to expand unchecked until it was impossible to tell the froth from the liquid. The rapid expansion in the Irish economy produces not only the physical straining, as we saw in the last chapter, but also a psychological one. People become euphoric, and act as though the boom will continue, no matter what numerous analogies and economic theory dictate must happen. They adjust their activity, and begin to consume in anticipation of further good times by borrowing irrationally, and not saving for a rainy day. Eventually, nearly everyone becomes intoxicated as everyone assumes that everyone else cannot be wrong. The banks lend the money, the consumers take it, who is to blame? I do not know, but I know who is going to pay for it in the end. The government basks in the glory and speaks of a shining future, the consumers spend even more furiously. How could everyone else be wrong?

No price is too high once everyone else is paying it. £100 for dinner for two, no problem, £150,000 for a small apartment, no problem. Wages are climbing and overtime abounds. Warning signs appear, they are ignored, nothing can stop us. Eventually most of the economy becomes engaged in a derivative of group think, the comparisons with the theoretical model are daunting.

A Perceived Immunity to Reality

The group's members believe that success can be achieved no matter how overwhelming circumstances are. I have spent many hours discussing the boom in Dublin with friends, acquaintances and even strangers. The vast majority are possessed of the opinion that nothing can go wrong, nothing will shake their confidence in this up-cycle. Many will not even admit to the small possibility that anything could go wrong. On the issue of house prices, (an entire chapter is dedicated to this topic later in the book), most consumers are possessed of the strangest belief: that house prices will climb up to a certain level, then go in a straight line forever. This belief structure dictates that no matter when you buy, you cannot lose, and the longer you delay, the more it, ultimately, costs you. This is not only an extremely dangerous path of thinking, it is also patently absurd. Never in the history of finance, has a commodity or investment product (including private residential housing) ever taken such a path. It is also impossible, because it breaks a pretty fundamental economic truth, you cannot have a risk free investment. If house prices are going to track such a path, then one could not lose money by buying into them. Unfortunately, risk and reward are inversely proportional.

House prices have cycled up and they will cycle down. They will, of course, cycle up again in a number of years, but they will fall by upto 40 per cent before that.

A Strong Offensive Against any Opponents

Opponents of the group are labelled as insipid, stupid or ignorant. A large number of people in Dublin have become very defensive to comparisons being made with other boom/bust situations. I read one article in an Irish paper that simply amazed me. It characterised anyone who was drawing comparisons with the UK housing boom, as a jack-the-lad who knows very little. It described how you could visit every pub in Dublin and find someone 'holding up the bar' pontificating about doom and gloom. The article was attempting to be balanced, but it produced two 'expert witnesses', an auctioneer and a stockbroker to feed more opiates to its readers, telling them that everything was fine.

What I found so ironic, was that the author of the article also had another piece in the same issue. The author was in the full heat of the hunt chasing around Dublin looking for a residence and was cataloguing it for the paper. In the article, she detailed how she found a nice little apartment for £100,000. In a subsequent article she discussed a flat over a chip shop for £130,000. The fact that flats of similar quality in London, New York, or Paris, are probably cheaper did not seem to raise any questions.

Those who Dissent are Pressured to Conform

Anyone inside the group who dissents is pressured to fall back into line by the rest of the group. I have had discussions with many people about the economy in Ireland and about house prices in Dublin in particular. In many cases, people are seized with a religious fervour to convert you to their way of thinking. I would sometimes try to change the subject after realising that the people were fairly sensitive about it, usually because they had just bought a house for £200,000. But to no avail, the topic would be returned to again and again, as they tried to get me to tell them that they paid the right price for their house. One argument even became a shouting match as I presented some of the arguments which I have presented in this book. I have now assumed the policy of never discussing house prices with anyone in Dublin.

Consolidated Justification

The group itself believes it cannot fail, this is because members are blinded to any potential signs of trouble. There is a recession in Asia, which could spread to the US and Germany but no one is concerned. The head of the Central Bank in the USA is worried, but no one in Ireland is. What would be the first type of spending to go if a downturn hits in the US? Luxuries. Is a new computer really necessary? Do we really need that holiday to Ireland? What would the effect be of a fall in new computers purchased, or a slow down in tourism, or a slow down in consumption of the many other products we sell to the US. What is the economy doing in the UK or Germany? Does anyone know the answers to these questions. Ireland is an extremely open economy. We are like a cat with a long tail in a room full of rocking chairs. We should be very worried about potential movements elsewhere, but we are not. For some reason, we think we are insulated from the outside world.

Mind Guards

Members of the group emerge to act as guardians of the groups norms. Information contrary to the position of the group, and criticism of the group, is held back from the other members. We all act as our own mind guards, skipping those articles we don't want to read, flipping channels when the programme on the health risks of smoking comes on. It is natural to avoid what we do not want to hear or see. The media in Ireland has also done a very good job whipping up the frenzy, and generally keeping reality at bay. I do not ask that the media preach 'doom and gloom', just that they preach some mild amount of caution.

Self-censorship by Group Members and Misinterpretation of Silence

The majority of people believe the hype, not only because they want to believe in it, but also because they believe everyone else believes in it. Again, it is important to stress that there is strong real economic growth in Ireland at the moment – more people have jobs, there is more money – the illusion is in the unrealistic expectation that such growth can be maintained and that a period of contraction will not follow such excessive growth.

On an individual basis, it is the critical altering in a person's perceptions that increases their expenditure and reduces their savings. People's perceptions are shaped by how prosperous they feel, which is based on the following information.

- How much money they are earning.

- How strong the economy is.

- How secure they feel in their job.

- What the government and 'experts' are telling them.

- What there friends and family and saying and doing.

- Their experience of boom/bust scenarios and the business cycle.

Based on this, it is not surprising that people are willing to spend more and save less. The more spending that occurs, the more demand is created, and it all goes round in one circle. It is all a self-fulfilling prophecy, up to a point. Eventually those on the outer edge of the boom extend themselves too much, and have to fold back their expenditure. This, combined with unforeseen economic events, then rolls back on other consumers in ever increasing waves.

An economist and a politician were arguing, the economist was trying to warn the politician of a possible downturn in the economy with little success. Finally he said, "The crux of the problem is the point where people's expectations of the future and the reality of that future separate." The line that tracks their expectations goes ever upwards and the line of reality tracks forward, or downwards, or even on a slower upward course. Eventually the two lines will have to be forced to meet, and the more separated they have become, the sharper the correction.

On a broader level, the natural tendency for people to promote positive and optimistic news, over pessimistic news, also helps to encourage the euphoria. When an economy is in the doldrums, the media becomes geared up to pushing the positive stories, as the news in general tends to be very disheartening. However, in boom this plays against the general good. It often involves the creative use of statistics.

In the boom in Dublin, such creative use of statistics has crept into the media. Not for any deceptive purpose, but just because people wish to hear good news, and so people wish to tell good news. It is nice to tell people happy news, and when it conform. to the general consensus, it makes everyone glow with the 'feel good' factor. Unfortunately, more good news than is justified can add to the euphoria and affect the decision making of consumers.

I was driving around Dublin one day last year, when I was home in Ireland for a visit. The news headlines blared out: "1,100 new jobs for Cork!!" This sounded fantastic, excellent news for the Cork region. The passenger in the car who knew of my slightly sceptical views, was ribbing me, "Look at how the economy is booming and you with your 'doom and gloom' economics." It was ten minutes before the expanded version of the story came on. The story explained that two different projects that were to create these jobs, and then almost as an afterthought they mentioned that the first operation, which was responsible for 300 of the jobs would create them over four years, and the second operation responsible for the remaining 800 jobs would create them over seven years! Compressing such news into one blitz headline creates a distorted perception of what is occurring.

If I asked you how much you earned, and you said £600,000, I would presume you are talking per annum, and that you were obviously a very prosperous and wealthy person. But what if you meant over the next 20 or 25 years, this would change matters completely. When you talk about figures, there must be a common time-frame, otherwise the figures are meaningless. A company that produces its accounts does so within a strict time framework, usually a year, they cannot bring sales forward into one year, to pad their figures. Such practices would be immediately rejected by an accountant or an auditor. Yet numbers are thrown about on the airways, as if no basic rules applied.

There is also a natural bias in jobs, that tends to distort figures simply because on one side of the equation you have job creations, and on the other, job losses. When a State organisation announces it has attracted new jobs, it wishes to put the best gloss on the facts and so announces everything in one go, with a big publicity flash. When a company is making job cuts, it talks about the absolute minimum numbers. One is maximised, one minimised and both nearly always refer to different time periods.

On the same day that the '1,100' jobs in Cork were announced, there was a small headline in a national paper that a company in Dublin was restructuring and making just over 100 people redundant. Most people who read the news and listened

to the radio would see 1,100 new jobs gained, 100 jobs lost, a net
gain of 1,000. They surmise that the economy is powering ahead,
and maybe it is, but you cannot tell from these figures. Companies
never announce job cuts seven years into the future, only those
over the immediate future. Companies cannot know the number
of jobs they may be shedding years in advance.

Let us assume then, for the sake of simplicity that 1,200 jobs
are to be created over eight years (adding 100 jobs to keep the
maths simple), with 200 for the first four years and 100 for each
of the last four years. None of the jobs will actually be created
until the year after the plant is announced, but the 100 redun-
dancies will occur in the very short-term.

	+	-
1998	0	100
1999	200	?
2000	200	?
2001	200	?
2002	200	?
2003	100	?
2004	100	?
2005	100	?
2006	100	?

The net effect this year between these two operations is a loss of
100 jobs. Furthermore, we have no information on what the company which sheds jobs, plans to do in the future. Maybe it thinks
it might need to make more people redundant but does not wish
to say so until it is sure. This is a very understandable and rational action. Yet on the other hand, how can the new factory
know it will be hiring a hundred people in five, six or seven year's
time. These job gains are based on the best case scenario, if things
go well and the market is strong, then we will need these people,
but this, of course, is never said. Within a reasonable degree of
certainty, all we can say is that this year 100 jobs are lost, and
over the next number of years, 1,100 more jobs may be created.

This is not to deny a general employment improvement in Ireland, unemployment is down and that is a great thing. We should,
however, only rely on current unemployment statistics and not
overdo the overly optimistic news because it can affect how people behave, and could even mask a downturn for some time before consumers could begin to take corrective action.

6

Boomtown

Everything in the world may be endured,
except continued prosperity.

Johann Wolfgang von Goethe

One day last year, I had arranged to meet someone in Dublin city centre, but I had arrived too early. I went to get a cup of coffee and read a newspaper to pass half an hour. It was about 3 pm, two premises refused to seat me because I only wanted a cup of coffee, when I did finally get a seat in small cafe, I was charged £1.50 for coffee in what looked to me to be a soup bowl. I was however, informed that this was the 'continental' way to drink coffee. I wondered which continent the waiter was referring to, but I kept quiet. It was, however, money well spent, not because of the coffee mind you, but because of the conversation I could not avoid overhearing.

Two women in their mid-twenties were both picking out cars to buy, and both were borrowing money to do so. Neither actually knew the price of the car, only what the monthly repayments were going to be. I think the figure was £199 a month. No term for the loan was ever discussed, was it for 48 months or was it a life-time commitment? Neither was an interest rate discussed, just the monthly payment, which both thought was, "brilliant". Other sundry costs such as insurance, motor tax, petrol, and parking, were never mentioned during the conversation either. After about fifteen minutes, a third woman joined the table and she interjected a mild bout of caution, "What if both of you lose your temporary jobs she asked?" The two other women looked at her and said, "Lose our jobs, haven't you read the paper; unemployment is over."

I have no idea what the occupations of these young women were, and maybe unemployment is over in their particular field, but I doubt it. Both the coffee for £1.50 and the unbridled optimism leading to possible financial overextension, reminded me of similar conversations I had heard in London in 1990. Just as the booming economy ended for London, and a hundred other up-cycles throughout history, so will it end for Dublin. This should not, necessarily, be looked at negatively, it will be good for some people and bad for others. Like most of life, those who are prepared will do well, and those who are not well-prepared will not do well. The economy will, of course, cycle upwards again a number of years later, as the over correction is corrected. Overall the economy in Ireland is improving, and over the long-term, it is on an upward path. But EMU-inspired interest rates have pulled us sharply from the path of reasonable growth, and that will be corrected before the long-term upward trend continues. There is a beautiful symmetry to most aspects of economics.

It is, however, necessary at the moment to deconstruct the Celtic Tiger myth, because it is this myth that is driving most of the irrational euphoria in Ireland. I must again stress, that I do not question the underlying growth that sparked our boom, it was the inability of our government to control the growth with interest rate rises, which has caused the intoxicated excesses in Dublin and other parts of the country. This has led to irrational behaviour by many consumers who are chanting the mantra of the Celtic Tiger as if it was a divine truth, rather than the catchy sound-bite it was supposed to be. The phrase 'Celtic Tiger' was coined by David McWilliams (although I have also heard someone else claim it). The Celtic Tiger story is that Ireland is now leaping ahead into the future, we have the highest growth in the industrialised world, we have practically no inflation, and foreign companies are flocking to our shores because we are a hi-tech and financial oasis in Europe. Furthermore, we have a capital city that is now, according to some newspaper columnists, one of the most cosmopolitan cities in the world. The international press are supposedly applauding our every move, and nothing can go wrong.

While everyone wishes to feel positive, and there are many reasons to be so, there are now even vastly greater reasons to be worried about the spread of the above myth. It has altered people's rational expectations which has, over the short-term, boosted growth, but the cost will be a sudden, sharp shock as people awaken from the dream.

The points I shall address are:

- the etymology of the phrase Celtic Tiger;

- the growth rate in Ireland;

- an explanation for the 'lack' of inflation;

- why foreign companies are coming here.

The phrase 'Celtic Tiger' was derived from Asian Tiger. This phrase referred to the marvellous economic progress that occurred in countries such as Thailand, Malaysia, Hong Kong and so on, in the late-1980s and first half of the 1990s. These growth rates were marvelled at, the stories were heralded throughout the world as shining examples of capitalist prosperity. Investors rushed to put money into their stock markets. This was, of course, facilitated and fuelled by stockbrokers, and investment houses, who benefited from the passage of the money through their hands, and who earned annual management fees. These brokers kept the pot boiling, and pumped positive stories into the media, most of which lapped it up like kittens. For example, Malaysia was held up as a shining example of the Asian Tigers. The tallest building in the world was built in Kuala Lumpur, the capital, and the prime minister of Malaysia announced that the country was going to become the technological centre for all of south-east Asia. Entire forests of paper were sacrificed in writing positive stories about Malaysia. Yet it all ended quickly. The currency was devalued rapidly, losing up to 70 per cent of its value, and foreign investment all but disappeared. Suddenly every financial paper and magazine was full of negative stories about Malaysia. How could things have changed so suddenly? The reality is probably that things didn't change much, just perceptions changed. The prime minister of Malaysia has now blamed some vast conspiracy by currency speculators and closed off the economy, making the local currency unconvertible.

On a wider scale, many Asian economies took a sharp turn for the worse and things have been going downhill rapidly. It now transpired that many problematic facts were glossed over by people who did not wish to be accused of 'doom and gloom' economics. There was much corruption in Asia, the infrastructure had problems handling the growth, some investors money was being squandered bidding up asset prices rather than really generating new production. The result in Asia overall, is now a large recession, property prices have fallen steeply, unemployment is soaring, and luxury items are being sold off by the owners who overestimated their ability to afford them.

There are, of course, many differences between Asia and Ireland. No two booms are ever the same, what is the same in all booms is the euphoria felt by most people throughout the affected economy, and this has quite often affected their ability to make rational decisions. It is vital to reiterate that no two boom/bust scenarios are the same, in the same way as no two car crashes are the same, the net results are, however, similar. It is easy to take one statistical figure and compare it with the boom in London, or Boston, or Hong Kong and demonstrate it is different in Ireland, so therefore the Irish economy is not in a boom/bust cycle. Using this analytical method, I could say that I saw three car crashes on various roads last year, and all coincidentally happened to involve white cars, so I am, therefore, immune from car crashes because I drive a red car.

The originator of the phrase 'Celtic Tiger', Mr McWilliams, is now urging strong caution. He said on a recent visit to Ireland, how he noticed strong comparisons with Boston (another boom/bust example). He now sees, "ominous parallels", between the Boston of his student days and Dublin of today. He fears a property price slump and recession. He charts many worrying parallels, from the explosion in the number of restaurants and cafes, to the dominance of hi-tech companies in the local economy. The originator of the 'Celtic Tiger' phrase is now waving a big warning flag but nobody is concerned. In fact, he was called an "outsider", no one called him an outsider when he said what they wanted to hear, but once he goes against the crowd, he is set upon. The 'Celtic Tiger' phrase has been repeated and repeated and repeated until we eat, sleep, and drink it. It has become the opium of the masses, soothing all worries as if it somehow allows an abrogation of personal financial responsibility.

We do have the highest growth rate in the Organisation of Economic Co-operation and Development, but if anyone boasts about this, it only demonstrates their superficial understanding of economics. The partial function of this book is to debunk any thought that rapid economic growth is a good thing, it is not. This is in no way a unique theory of mine, in fact I have yet to see any economics book that says anything other than what I am saying. If someone finds a book that says growth of over 10 per cent in an economy such as ours is desirable, I shall be very interested to see it. Excessive growth causes problems, not only with the physical infrastructure that cannot expand quickly enough, but with the inhabitants in the economy. It distorts psychological perceptions, and encourages many people and businesses to abandon prudence in the belief that such growth can be maintained indefinitely. Excessive growth will also create inflation which, eventually, causes many other distortions in an economy.

The myth that there is no inflation in the Irish economy is one that has endured for quite some time. Even our own Finance Minister seems to believe there is no inflation in Ireland. Let us initially define inflation. A dictionary definition describes it as a "general increase in prices". That seems fairly simple, however when the government speaks of inflation, they speak of the consumer price index (CPI). The CPI is a weighted index of various items which, the Central Statistics Office[1] has deemed, reflect the average household in Ireland. There are, however, a few flaws with using the CPI to represent inflation.

- It is a nationwide average and may actually be representative of very few real people. It is, in essence, an average, a very sophisticated and well-structured average, but the CPI is just one figure. We could easily, for example, compute what the average shoe size is for men in Ireland. Let us say that the figure is calculated at shoe size 9½. This would be an accurate average, but it gives very little information about the distribution of shoe sizes and it certainly could not be used to make shoes for everybody. In fact, you might find that there are an equal number of 9s and 10s in the country, and if you gave everyone size 9½ shoes, they would fit no one well. Thus, there may be large numbers of people experiencing strong inflation, and many experiencing no inflation, or even deflation, which leads to the next point.

- No figures are issued for Greater Dublin, which has become an economy inside the economy of Ireland. It is the heart of the furnace, where a large proportion of the population lives, and yet there are no CPI figures for Dublin. I asked the Central Statistics Office specifically about this matter and received the answer, "No, we do not have regional CPI figures." Although I presume they must have the raw

---

1.   Using the 'Household Budget Survey' conducted every five years.

data with which to calculate them. If the government is willing to carve up the country for EU grants into prosperous, and not so prosperous, then I do not see why they should not issue regional CPI figures. We can only assume that if house prices have been rising much faster in Dublin, then other prices may also be rising faster. Although I must stress I have no proof of such a correlation between house prices and general price levels, it is an assumption based on my own experiences with prices in Dublin.

- The CPI does not include house prices, and there are many valid theoretical arguments for this. The CSO even has an excellent release which explains their reasons for this. The reason is that houses are an asset, as opposed to a consumer item, and I fully understand these arguments. The result is that there can be massive asset inflation in Ireland, with new homes moving beyond the affordability of many people, but the CPI figure cannot reflect this. On another front, the CPI does include private rents in the 'housing' category. But this total category has only risen 4.9 per cent between November 1996 and September 1998. Anyone paying rent in Dublin, or in fact, in any other city in the country, would find this a nearly impossible figure to believe. I would like to know which apartments the CSO uses, and where exactly they are located. This all reinforces my opinion that the CPI is using a basket of reference points, far from what a large segment of people are experiencing in real life.

- On a technical point, I would like to know how does the CPI account for price rises such as the taxi driver who overcharged me £4? If it was not on the meter, I doubt the Revenue Commissioners heard about it, and it is even less likely the CSO found out about it. As the economy expands rapidly, how does the CSO account for this type of grey-economy? How many plasterers, carpenters and plumbers have increased their prices but not reported them?

- What sampling techniques do the CSO employ? By this I mean, do they sample the same place every time, or do they alter where they sample, or increase the number of samples to include new premises. What is the lifestyle they are measuring, that of an average 40 year old married person from an average county in Ireland, or a twenty-something yuppie from Dublin who rents his accommodation?

The above questions are, of course, 'loaded' and unfair to a certain degree. I know the CPI has to choose an average, and I know they are bending over backwards to be representative of everyone, but this is the problem. The strength of the CPI is its weakness, it is a broad average of a basket of goods in Ireland as a whole. It cannot, and does not, pretend to serve the purposes of any individual person. It does, however, serve the purpose of the government to claim that inflation is low. The de facto evidence of the CPI's 'inaccuracy' is the very activity of the government. The government, when pressured, is willing to make large pay settlements to those who have the economic muscle to rock the boat, but will still claim to everyone else that inflation is 3 per cent. The government set up the Bacon Commission to find out why the prices of houses were rising rapidly, but that is asset inflation of course, a different kind of inflation. The Gardai were driven, for the first time in the history of the State, to go on strike. I accept that they did not technically go on strike, but the 'blue flu' was either a medical anomaly or disguised industrial action. The fact that Gardai felt forced to take action is a clear indication that not many people are willing to accept this 3 per cent inflation figure. The nurses followed suit, as will many others. Every person in the economy is able to gauge approximately what their own inflation rate is, and will react accordingly. Each person has a different basket of goods, and so each has their own inflation rate. If you are single and live in rented accommodation in central Dublin and socialise quite often, then you are going to have a completely different inflation rate from a married couple who bought their house ten years ago in County Kerry.

The government's stance does, however, achieve one important thing, the drumbeat that inflation is 3 per cent could possibly be soothing many people who might otherwise begin to anticipate inflation. Once people begin to anticipate inflation, inflation (including the CPI version) will really begin to take off.

Our Central Bank is strongly urging the Finance Minister to control fiscal expenditure in some attempt to control future inflation, but Mr McCreevy knows better. In an interview, the Finance Minister explained that Ireland was in a new economic

'mode' and that we can have steamroller growth but practically
no inflation; he further stated that, "Traditional economic theory
does not apply to Ireland." Maybe Mr McCreevy knows something that many others don't, and I will await his paper in the
economics journals with eagerness. I might suggest a name for
his paper, it could be called "Monetary Policy: Who Needs One?",
or maybe "Central Banks: An Unnecessary Financial Burden".
Yes, I am being facetious, but I just cannot understand how Mr
McCreevy can believe this. During every boom in history, there
is always a general consensus that a 'new era' has arrived, that
a 'historic shift' has occurred and the country has moved beyond
the norm. But for a Finance Minister to be telling all and sundry
that a few hundred years of economic theory can be thrown out
the window, is an amazing statement. Mr McCreevy then goes
on to state that there is no major inflation in the economy. If this
is so, why is 'his' government giving double digit pay awards to
many civil servants? Why can no ordinary couple afford a house
in Dublin? Why are officials contemplating a 22 per cent rise in
old-age pensions? Why are these events occurring if there is no
inflation? I am, of course, assuming the dictionary definition of
inflation. We can enter into a game of Clintonesque semantics,
where we argue over what inflation is, and whether the CPI is
measuring inflation. I am, however, sure that Mr McCreevy
knows best, he is after all, the Minister for Finance.

In order that I am not accused of using selective extracts, Mr
McCreevy further stated in the same interview, "We should be
cautious, what I am trying to do is to have a reasonable level of
growth and prosperity in the long-term rather than have tremendous peaks and tremendous valleys." Yet this only confuses
matters more for me – am I to infer from this that Mr McCreevy
thinks 10 per cent plus is a reasonable level of growth? When he
speaks of tremendous peaks and tremendous valleys, is he saying
that we are on some tremendous peak already, or we might be
on one? And if so, when does he expect the tremendous valley
to occur?

Foreign companies are flocking to Ireland's shores for many
reasons. The main ones are the flexibility of our workers, our EU
membership, lower labour costs and a highly skilled and educated population. Ireland has one of the most accomplished and
able workforces in Europe, and it is something of which we should
be proud, our human resources have always been our greatest
asset. Yet there are threats to our popularity as a long-term base
for some operations. These threats come from:

- **European bureaucracy**: Ireland, compared to most of the rest of Europe, has an extremely flexible workforce. While Irish employers may complain about the regulations surrounding workers, I can assure you that German managers dream about the kind of flexibility we have. France recently passed a mandatory 35-hour work week into law. German employers have to pay nearly 80 per cent on top of an employee's salary in PRSI-type benefits. Sick leave and maternity benefits are at near utopian levels in many European countries, and employees, once hired, are difficult to shed. These are just a few examples of the costs facing business people in many European countries.

- The view of our government, and most Irish people, is the Anglo-Saxon view of capitalism. In continental Europe, the social-market view of capitalism is predominant. Whereas we realise the function of a business is to make profit, in most of Europe, the function of business is quite often seen as an employer of people. This is a subtle, but important difference which burdens many firms with enormous social responsibility that is really not theirs.

  Most Irish people do not realise how flexible they are when compared to mainland Europeans, which is the attraction to many foreign companies who want to get manufacturing plants inside 'fortress Europe'. Yet, the EU is slowly pushing employment laws and other regulations upon us. The UK is fighting these, as we are, but they are probably acting as a blocking guard for us at this stage. Yet, many inflexibilities may eventually be forced upon us, and soon the difference between us and mainland Europe, may be very small. The German government is already complaining about Ireland's 'on sale' corporate tax rate. If Germany could use the EU eventually to force this up to German levels over twenty years, it would be interesting to know how many companies would be inclined to come here, or even stay here. We must realise that what makes us such an excellent base, is, in part, the difference we have with other EU countries, not the similarities and, after all, the goal of the EU is harmonisation.

- **EU expansion**: the EU is expanding east, it will not be long before Hungary, and probably Poland and the Czech Republic, will be in the EU. It is important to realise that these are 'central European' countries and not eastern Europe. It might be easy to dismiss them as 'backward', but I can assure you that they are not. Countries, such as Hungary, were power houses of the continent before communism burdened them. They have now been progressing very quickly since the 'fall of the wall', and will soon be ready for EU entry. Foreign companies may soon have a less expensive labour pool to utilise inside EU borders. As unemployment falls here, and our standard of living rises, then so does the cost to employ us. The very act of becoming more prosperous, means we are more expensive. Central European countries are still far below European average levels of income, which means not only will they get the grant money we used to get, they will also get some of the jobs we have now, or may get.

It will be important to maintain our technological and educational advantage so we can keep the edge we have. If all our factories do is put part A into part B, then they will be gone to Hungary once it is in the EU.

We pride ourselves on the calibre of the people we produce, but we are not as advanced as we think. A recent report from the National Adult Literacy Agency, stated that 25 per cent of the overall population are functionally illiterate. In the critical 15 to 16 year age bracket this figure is 17 per cent, and that is worrying for a country that boasts about its education levels. I found these figures startling and a far cry from what I have always believed. Yet, it was further reinforced by a report from the Organisation of Economic Co-operation and Development, which indicated that Irish literacy levels are the second lowest in the whole continent of Europe.

While we have strong economic advantages, the myth of the Celtic Tiger must be eradicated or we will wake up and find many foreign companies leaving Ireland and heading abroad. We cannot let a glib phrase immunise us from reality. Ireland has a great long-term future if only we do not become drunk on success. Unfortunately, at the moment, the economy is burning bright, instead of glowing constantly. This situation is, unfortunately, only going to be corrected by a sharp shock. The test of the tiger is how well it will extract itself from a mild downturn in the economy.

7

Credit

He is rich who owes nothing.

French proverb

The fuel of any boom is excessive demand, and demand is created by spending. Spending occurs because people earn more, save less or borrow more. While there is always more earning in a boom, it is always accompanied by more borrowing and less saving. The hangover created by this borrowing and lower savings, is what causes and maintains a recession after a boom has ended. This simplifies matters slightly, but it gets across the important point that a lot of demand, in an up-cycle exists because people choose to spend money, which they would otherwise save in leaner times, or borrow money that they would not have borrowed before.

Let's start with some very basic questions.

- Why do people decide to borrow money?

- What do people borrow this money for?

- Why do people save money?

Why do people borrow money? This question has the very simple answer – because they want it, but unfortunately that is not sufficient or really accurate. People borrow money in order to bring forward consumption from some date in the future. If I wish to 'consume' a car, I have two choices, assuming I don't have the money on hand, I can save up and buy it at some point in the future, or, alternatively, I can borrow the money, have the car now, and repay the capital sum along with interest. The interest is payment for the use of the money for the period of the loan. Borrowing is a speculative bet on your own future, you are gambling that you will be able to earn enough money to repay the loan. The overall demand for credit is a function of two main factors: the confidence of the person in the stability of their income stream and the cost of credit, i.e. the interest rate.

The more confident people become in their jobs, the economy and the future of that economy, then the more confident they will become of their stream of income to repay any borrowings.

The cost of credit is the interest rate charged. Credit has a demand curve like any other product, and it follows the normal pattern. The lower the price is, the more demand there will be for it, and the more of it will be demanded.

The question of what people borrow money for is, in many cases, a long way from what people should borrow money for. It would be a general opinion when I venture to say that borrowing should be somewhat productive. If you are going to bring forward consumption, then you should get continuing utility from the item you buy with the money. A house, for example, may be considered a wise investment for many people. Historically it appreciates in value, you eliminate the cost of paying rent, and on the intangible side of the equation it gives people pride and a stake in the community. On the other end of the spectrum, it may be considered imprudent to borrow money to go on a holiday or to have an expensive wedding. The utility is consumed fairly quickly and you are left with debt. Although, again, this is a subjective commentary not an objective one. In a free society, people can do as they wish with their money, be it borrowed or earned.

Saving money is, by definition, deferring consumption, it is the opposite of borrowing. People save money in order to allow for unforeseen future circumstances, a rainy day, or for a known future need at a fixed date in the future, such as a child's education. The other important factor that determines if people save or not, is the interest rate on offer for saving. The lower the interest rate, the less likely the person is to save. It is a standard supply curve, the lower the interest rate on offer for people's money, then the less money people will save. There will, of course, always be a fixed group of people who will borrow or save no matter what – the important group are those that alter their behaviour because of altering circumstances.

On the opposite side of this whole equation are the financial institutions. Whereas you can freely decide to save money, it requires a bank, or other financial institution, to loan you money in order for you to borrow it. It is this loan approval process that plays a significant part in the amount of money in circulation in the economy. Any institution that lends money to consumers, has a hand in controlling the quantity of money in circulation. However, an excess of lending ultimately leads to a recession, because the quality and quantity of money loaned out exceeds prudence, and it must, eventually, be paid back. Borrowing is simply consumption brought forward, if too much is brought forward, then it distorts the current, and future, demand and supply patterns in the economy. Ultimately, those who borrowed excessively must cut their spending to repay the debt and this starts a downward spiral in demand. Not only is newly borrowed money absent from demand, but the consumer is paying back previously borrowed money with current income. In Ireland, it is clear that credit has expanded and that people are entering into, and being drawn into, unwise credit commitments. There are two clear intertwined areas of the credit explosion and I will discuss each separately. The first is consumer borrowing and the latter is business borrowing.

As we have seen above, consumers will want to borrow money based on their own perceived ability to pay it back. However, that perception becomes distorted during a boom. It is, of course, a 'chicken and egg' situation. Initial borrowing creates more demand for goods, which creates the positive economic environment, which creates further demand for borrowing and further demand for goods. Debts slowly edge up as people become more and more optimistic, the more optimistic they become about the future, the more they are willing to borrow based on their future income. In 1955, Geoffrey Moore, a business cycle analyst stated that the signs which precede a recession are clear to see, if only we looked. The four signs he said are:

- a rapid expansion in the volume of credit and debt;

- vigorous competition among lenders for new business;

- relaxation of credit terms and lending standards;

- a rapid and speculative increase in the prices of investment goods, such as real estate.

In Ireland, every single one of these is visible for all to see. Borrowing has expanded from almost every single source. The artificial reduction in interest rates forced upon us, has driven borrowing wild. As history demonstrates, banks are foolish in deciding who to lend to in booms, as they tend to become as intoxicated as the borrowers. Any control mechanism is torn out from the system, and it just spirals upward. It must, of course, collapse under its own weight once any minor disruption alters people's perceptions. And history shows that something will always turn up. In hindsight, it is easy to say it was an unforeseen event, but the fact that something is going to go wrong should not be unforeseen.

What is even more worrying, is what borrowed money is being used for in Ireland. Gone are the days when borrowing was reserved for houses or house extensions, education and cars necessary to transport people to and from work. The explosion in credit now means that every store in the country is lending for almost anything, credit cards have proliferated and term loans are being thrown at people. Rather than wise investments, loans are now used for consumption purposes and sundry, unnecessary goods. People who see prosperity around them want to be part, and even expect to be part of it, so they borrow in anticipation of the good fortune spreading to them. The banks don't care any more what you do with the money, and even if they do, you can lie to them and get away with it! Why? Because they are now competing with each other.

In recent years, things were pretty much divided in Ireland. The building societies lent for mortgages and the banks stayed with business and short-term financing for consumers. There is, of course, nothing wrong with competition, but it is the move from regulated to deregulated that causes ripples. Most of the lines of financial demarcation have now been crossed – you can now get a mortgage from a bank and borrow for a car with a building society. There are radio advertisements competing for the loan business, but quite often they are encouraging borrowing from people too weak to resist temptation. An increase in competition has led to an increase in borrowing and a lowering of the overall standards for loans.

The lowering of the standards for borrowing of all kinds, has specifically affected the mortgage business. It is less than ten years since building societies required that you save for a fixed period of time with them in order to buy a house, the logic being that if you could save consistently, then you could repay consistently. This was a very shrewd yardstick to weed out lower quality borrowers. Now you can walk in the door of most building societies and banks and get a loan without a long-term financial history with the institution. There is an entire chapter on housing prices in Dublin later in this book, so I will not go into it too much here, but one instance will demonstrate the laxness of lenders. I know, personally, of one person who wanted a mortgage, but did not have the deposit, so he simply got a unsecured term loan in one institution, lodged it in the other as his deposit and got his mortgage. When comparing the Irish boom with the UK boom, many commentators have frequently pointed out that 100 per cent mortgages were being handed out by UK financial institutions. It is claimed that this is not occurring in Ireland, and this is used this point to support the thesis that the Irish boom is somehow more rational than the UK boom. This is a relatively minor point, but I should straighten the record. Just because one institution does not lend you the entire 100 per cent, does not mean that a 100 per cent mortgage situation is not occurring. If you are borrowing the deposit equivalent to 10 per cent of the loan, and getting a 90 per cent mortgage based on this, then you are getting a 100 per cent mortgage. In fact, you could then probably go out and buy the furniture and consumer appliances with store credit and effectively end up with a 110 per cent 'mortgage'. Although I have personal knowledge of only one case such as this, I have been told of others. Considering that this is something people would not broadcast, I suspect that based on my small sample such borrowing practices may be more widespread than people might think.

A friend of mine told me that his bank sent him a letter offering him a term loan for any purpose he wanted. He did not need a loan for any reason, so he ignored it. A week later he received a phone call from the same bank, asking him had he received the letter, when he replied that he had no need for the loan, the bank employee started to press him, mildly, to take it. The employee, who obviously had a quota to make up, or who was working on some commission basis, started suggesting things he could spend the borrowed money on. Absolute madness!

In another example of the laxness with which borrowing is viewed, I saw an advertisement placed by a large garage in a national magazine. It quotes not actual prices for cars, but the repayment per week. There is no mention of a capital sum, interest rate, repayment period, etc. Just the different cars you can have and the repayment per week. This kind of credit offering is worrying. Sugar coating credit can only lead to financial difficulties for people.

It is impossible to ascertain, with the above kind of lending

practices, where the money is going, all I know is that it is unlikely to be long-term enduring investments. In Ireland, and
Dublin particularly, it is obvious that real estate has risen along
with other investment assets. The increased ability to borrow
money to bid for a fixed number of assets, means that the price
of those assets will go up, be they shares or apartments. The fall
in the return on savings also encourages investors to try to find
investment vehicles that will deliver a higher rate of return. This
desire has led to speculative activity in the asset market that
would not otherwise have occurred. Although I do not know of
any, there are always large investment scams in an up-cycle, as
those who are not earning the large salaries try to get in on the
boom with get-rich-quick schemes. The sign that the top of a
boom has been reached, or is about to be reached, is quite often
the failure of large investment schemes, that have sucked in a lot
of money with promises of large returns.

If, in 1955, analyst Geoffrey Moore could clearly see the signs
of recession, then why are the banks and building societies not
recognising what they are doing? This is a very good question,
and the answer is probably that the bankers themselves give into
temptation and euphoria like everyone else. Bankers are, after
all, human like the rest of us, and susceptible to normal human
emotions. Furthermore, they are under intense competitive pressure to loan out money. Japanese, UK and German bankers have
all been lulled into a false sense of security on a massive scale at
one time or another. So what makes us think our bankers would
be any different? Just because a bank is giving you a loan, you
should not infer that this is some kind of approval of the act of
borrowing this money. For many years we relied on our banks
and building societies to hold our hands and try to keep us out
of hot water. Those days are long gone.

Once loans begin to go bad, the banks will realise their exposure and cut credit with a pair of shears. This process is known
as a credit squeeze – once they are burnt, banks pull back quickly.
The credit squeeze, of course, draws money from the economy,
escalating whatever the downturn, no matter what initiated it.

The government has not instigated any study to determine if
excessive borrowing is occurring. I realise that we are all responsible for our own actions, but if the government deems it
necessary to dictate to us that we cannot have another pint of
beer in a pub after a certain time, you might think they would
attempt to limit people borrowing money. They cannot, of course,

use the standard tool of higher interest rates, but there are other methods.

The simplest, and most effective, method was suggested in Chile in 1996 when the Finance Minister became extremely worried about credit expansion. His idea was based on a central registry of all credit balances outstanding for each citizen. Information on the outstanding balances of store cards, credit cards, mortgages, car loans, term loans, etc. is stored centrally on a computer. It was a very simple idea, but it would go a long way in terms of putting the brakes on in Ireland. Any lender could instantly see the overall outstanding balance of a potential borrower with one quick phone call. Borrowers may simply lie when attempting to over-borrow, or may not even be fully aware themselves of how much they owe. The government need not define any limit to borrowing, it could just let this information be available to all financial institutions on request, and let them decide. A symmetrical information distribution can only lead to better decisions. The actual setting up of such a service would make borrowers think twice before unnecessary borrowing, because it would indicate that the government is taking matters seriously. The very fact that we could be taking lessons in financial prudence from South American countries, should be setting alarm bells off in all quarters of our economy.

Businesses can equally borrow too much money, but for different reasons. During a strong up-cycle, the business community faces some tough decisions. The main dilemma revolves around expansion. Let us take an example to demonstrate this.

Assume that there are two brothers, one owns a restaurant, and the other owns a brewery. Business for both starts to grow very quickly in the boom in Ireland. Both brothers are turning away customers, and this is not in their nature. They realise that their businesses are losing potential revenue, and this potential business may be an inducement for someone else to open in competition with them. Both of them decide to discuss how they can best expand. The brother, who owns the restaurant, realises that he can knock out a wall and make his floor surface bigger and move his kitchens into the basement. The cost is not too expensive as it does not require any major redevelopments or purchases of extra property. His largest expenditure will be the salaries of two more waiters and an extra chef to deal with the extra demand.

The brother who owns the brewery is not so lucky. If he wants to expand, he needs to buy a new set of brewing equipment, which will automatically double his capacity. This is more than he will need, but with the rate of growth, he will probably grow into the potential supply. He will also be able to extract larger profit per unit because of economies of scale, and if need be, he can lower his price per unit if he does experience competition. He must borrow money from the bank to buy this equipment, but rates are low, the banks are eager to lend, and he has a good track record.

The essential difference in these two cases is in how they expanded. The restaurant has incurred variable expenses in expanding and the brewery has incurred fixed expenses.

If the economy takes a downturn, the restaurant can immediately pull back by firing the waiters and chef, the brewery however, has made capital expenditure and owes fixed repayments to a bank every month. It cannot avoid this, the equipment is specially built and installed and cannot be returned. Fixed outgoings can sink a business because they are not varying with turnover. No matter what business the brewery does, the repayments must be made.

Even if neither of the brothers expanded, other businesses would open to meet the supply and the effect could be the same. More money would be borrowed to set up to service growing demand. In the down-cycle, many of these new businesses fail, and many older businesses drown in debt. The commercial world is littered with businesses that overextended in a boom and could not contract fast enough.

In Ireland, both commercial and private lenders must clearly lay out various financial scenarios before borrowing. And not just the most optimistic ones. What would happen if you lost your job, or if business dropped 20 per cent instead of rising by 20 per cent? Precautions must be taken to ensure that you are prepared for all reasonable expectations. Borrowing money is a major decision whether you are an individual or a corporate entity.

8

The Housing Market

> *How many legs does a dog have if you*
> *call the tail a leg? Four.*
> *Calling a tail a leg doesn't make it a leg.*

Abraham Lincoln

I wrestled with the quotation to introduce this chapter, there are so many to choose from that comment on the ability of people to convince themselves of something that is clearly illogical. The Dublin housing crisis could probably be ended tomorrow if you replaced every single person in Dublin with someone else from another part of the world. A ridiculous suggestion, but the point I am trying to make is that the panic in Dublin, and that is what it is, is mostly in the minds of people. A fresh batch of residents in Dublin would quite possibly view matters in a completely different light. Dublin's, and by contagion Ireland's, housing boom is as classic an asset price bubble as I have seen to date. It could, and I predict will, be used in economic text books as a true example of how prices can become distorted by human perceptions.

The single sign that finally brought home to me the level of irrationality reached in the 'Dublin' housing market, was an advertisement/article that appeared in one of our national newspapers last summer. This advertisement/article concerned a house in County Carlow that was described as 60 miles from the capital. It looked like a quaint cottage-type house, and the description was beautiful. If I lived in Carlow, I might be interested. But it was being advertised for people working in Dublin, with the phrase, "a realistic trek for the new generation of east coast commuters". That one phrase symbolised not only the skills of the salesperson who wrote it, but the levels that housing had reached in Greater Dublin. That someone would even consider travelling such a distance each day, seems like insanity. Yet the auctioneers phrase makes it look almost attractive and fashionable. You too, could be one of the, "new generation of east coast commuters". It sounds like an ad for a soft drink. The price quoted was "offers in excess of £115,000", which presumably means they are looking for £130,000.

The reality of paying £130,000 to live 60 miles from Dublin should be explored a little further. I have been reasonably assured by a number of people from that area, that the realistic trekking time from this location in County Carlow to the centre of the capital, is at best, one and a half hours at busy times. I could call it two hours, but I do not want to be accused of exaggeration. That is fifteen hours a week commuting to and from Dublin for work, and let's assume you make one trip on the weekend for social reasons. That is eighteen hours a week driving to the city, and 720 miles (or 1,100 kilometres)

per week on your odometer. Assuming that you get 25 miles per gallon for a mixture of country and city driving, you will consume almost 29 gallons (or 130 litres) of fuel per week. The cost of that fuel would be, at 65 pence per litre, just slightly under £85 per week. If you allow a figure of 10 pence per mile depreciation[1] and maintenance, this amounts to another £70 per week. Combining the two figures, you arrive at £155 per week in transport costs, which is £670 per calendar month, or £8,000 per year, after tax that is.

Let's assume you get a 'bargain' and buy the house for the base price of £115,000, then your mortgage over twenty years at 6.5 per cent, would be just over £850 per month. If rates fall much further then your mortgage would almost equal your transport costs.

In economic terms, I could probably make a reasonable argument, that if the current owners were working in Dublin, then they should, in fact, pay you for taking the house off their hands. I jest, but not by much. I am, of course, completely ignoring the costs of a person wasting their time sitting in a car. Assuming the person is a professional, then his or her time would be worth at an absolute minimum of £15 per hour which adds up to another £975 per month in opportunity cost to sit in a car for

---

1.   Putting 40,000 miles a year on a car just driving to work, will mean you are going to have high maintenance costs and probably be replacing the car every third year.

fifteen hours a week. Although it cannot be proved that the £975 is a real cost, it is a notional cost of what they could earn if they used this time productively. There would also be broader costs on a family of someone leaving for work at 6.30 am and returning at 8 pm for the foreseeable future, but these are impossible to quantify.

In order to become one of the "new generation of east coast commuters", you have to earn £14,000 for the commuting costs, and possibly forgo another £11,500 in potential earnings. That anyone thinks such a preposition merits buying advertising space is a clear indication that the property market has become highly irrational. I have, for the sake of simplicity, made the assumption that one person in the family is working, the reality is that probably both partners would have to be working, which makes the figures even more absurd.

Yes, this is an extreme case, but it is a real case and indicative of the upper end of the irrational frenzy. Most property supplements are, however, full of houses far from Dublin, available for prices well into the six figures. Houses anywhere near the city centre, start at £200,000 unless you want to live in an area where your car won't be outside your door in the morning. How did the situation arrive at this in Dublin? Well, there is a dividing line between the two sets of factors, the first set are physical and realistic, the second are psychological.

Firstly, I shall examine the practical factors. There are some definite physical reasons why house prices rose in Dublin. These are:

- interest rates;
- increased real demand.

For the vast majority of homeowners, the only way they can afford to buy houses is to borrow money. The amount they can borrow is a function of the repayments they can afford. Although the building society still states that it is adhering to the fixed 'multiple of income' formula, I don't believe that this could be the case. If, for example, you borrowed £60,000 five years ago, you would have been paying 9 per cent, and your monthly repayments over twenty years would be £540. With interest rates at 6 per cent, today you could make repayments with this £540 on a £75,000 loan over the same period. So a reduction in interest rates allows a commensurate rise in people's ability to borrow.

Because everyone can do this, and they are bidding in the short-term for the same supply of houses, then the prices will rise. Anything that affects everyone, will put the price up in the short-term. If the government increased the first-time buyers' grant to £10,000, then all that would happen is that people could bid £10,000 more in the auction houses and the prices would rise by £10,000. Giving everyone an equal extra sum of money just creates asset inflation, when supply cannot rise. People who are desperate to buy, will give every penny they can to a seller, so the more money you give them, the more they will give away. The reduction in interest rates allows people to afford to borrow more, and the more they can borrow, the higher they all will bid.

It is quite easy to prove that the financial institutions are lending more than the fixed multiple of people's incomes. If you are allowed to borrow 2.5 times one salary, plus 1 times a second salary, then the maximum a couple earning the average industrial wage of £16,000 per year could borrow, would be £56,000. A professional couple both earning £25,000 could borrow up to £87,500. A well-paid, professional couple both earning £35,000 each could borrow a maximum £122,500. The last couple might be able to buy something in the Greater Dublin area, but the other two would not have much chance. Yet houses have been bought by many people over the last two years for well in excess of these three salary brackets, so 'something does not gel' as our American cousins would say.

What has probably been happening to increase the amount being lent to house buyers, is a mixture of a number of factors.

- The lender has been looking at the ability of the borrower to make a certain monthly repayments, rather than using the 'fixed multiple' formula.

- Salaries have been rising over the last number of years.

- The definition of what is acceptable as salary has expanded, allowing overtime and bonuses, if they were occurring regularly.

- Lenders have been taking into account such things as lodgers paying part of the mortgage.

- The borrower has been exaggerating, or lying, as to what they are earning.

The impact of lower interest rates also drives up demand from another source, investors. Those with money in the financial institutions have been getting a lower and lower return, and so may be tempted to take the money out to buy property. With rents rising rapidly, investors may believe that they will get a better return from rental income. The sharp rise in property prices may also attract those who jump in, to try to benefit from any further capital gain.

The physical factors that are affecting demand began with a demographic blip in young prospective buyers coming on to the market. It was followed by a general economic increase in activity, which attracted more people to Dublin and encouraged emigrants to return. These are all realistic increases in demand. However, as with many other bull markets, the initial demand was followed by psychologically induced demand.

As prices began to rise in Dublin, people began to sit up and take notice of the housing market. People began to worry that there might be no houses for them when the time came for them to buy. A crowd will always attract more buyers. Other buyers started to bring forward decisions to buy, and this, of course increased the price as demand rose and supply could not react in the short-term. The further prices went up, the more people panicked and rushed into the market, and the more sellers began to hold back property awaiting even more rises. People became less and less rational as they saw everyone else buy and became afraid they would be left out in the cold. The conversations in every social gathering was housing, "Oh, we just got in, you better hurry." The frenzy drove prices up in leaps and bounds, people became less rational, and you eventually had advertisements like the one for the house in County Carlow. An entire mythology has grown up from little seeds to great oak trees, and have been given credence by people who should know better. These myths have, of course, a basis of truth in them, but they do nothing but distort reality. The main misconceptions are that:

- there is a shortage of land to build houses on in Dublin, and soon it will run out;

- people are pouring into the country, and there is no emigration anymore, so supply is going to be continuously drowned out by more demand;

- everyone who owns a house is richer today than they were two years ago.

I will start with the strangest argument about Dublin, i.e. that there is somehow a shortage of land in Dublin. I do not know where to start with this argument, it is so ludicrous that I will confine my discussion to two simple points.

The first point is that if land is running out in Dublin, then the physical size of any city could not go above the current size of Dublin without encountering such supply of land problems. You need only take a trip to cities like London to see that this is not the case. Greater London contains about 9 million people. It is true that Dublin faces the sea, so there is about 50 per cent less land available, but still, half of one side of London contains 4.5 million people. So it must be physically possible to fit large numbers of people into a large metropolitan area without resorting to massive amounts of apartment type housing. Liverpool or Manchester are closer in size to Dublin and neither have any major property crisis at the moment. They are large cities with low property prices and no panic. I could name many cities facing the sea, that have more than a million people and a larger number of inhabitants, but a lower cost of housing. So simple physical evidence tells us that it is possible to fit millions of people comfortably into an urban conurbation without any panic over running out of land. It may require a better transport system, but that is nothing to do with land, that is an infrastructure problem with just takes time to address.

The second argument is a simpler one. Put a compass in a map of Dublin and draw a circle 25 miles out. Now let's remove 50 per cent of that space because Dublin faces the sea. That leaves you with $(3.14 \times 25^2 \times .5)$ this is equal to 918 square miles. Let us further assume that 95 per cent of this space is already occupied, structurally unsuitable for building, or required for green areas, wild life reserves or whatever. This leaves us with 49 square miles of land that must be able to be obtained for building houses on. It might be green field or brown field sites, but it cannot be an unreasonable assumption to assume that 5 per cent of land in a large radius of Dublin could, physically, be built upon. If there are 640 acres to a square mile, and ten houses per acre, then there is room for approximately 300,000 new houses in Dublin within the 25 mile radius. Now I accept this is an estimate, but it is a reasonably educated guess, I have been around Dublin enough to know that 5 per cent land is not an unrealistic figure. Being 25 miles from the city centre may seem a lot, but the world does not revolve around the city centre. Suburban living means you live near your place of work, and rarely come to a city centre.

The problem with the supply of land in Dublin is not a purely physical one. The shortage is in the supply of zoned and serviced land, and this is the bottleneck in the whole supply chain. Re-zoning land to residential use is simply an artificial mechanism that restricts the supply of land. I understand that there are many planning laws, etc. to be heeded, but from what is being revealed day to day in the newspapers, the key to getting land zoned in Ireland in recent history has been 'payments'. Payments is of course a euphemism for bribes. (I do not understand why no one in the media is willing to use the word bribe. If what was going on in Ireland was happening in any other country, then the word bribe would be used liberally. I presume our libel laws are so onerous that we use words like 'payments' and 'contributions' out of fear.) Whatever we want to call these 'payments', the power to convert the use of land is an artificial mechanism that will eventually give way to demand levels. The public and media are watching the re-zoning process like hawks, and developers are probably much more likely to go public now if they are asked for any 'contributions' to party political coffers for planning approval. I think the zoning bottleneck will be breached, and quickly. It is amazing what politicians can do when you light a fire under them.

The real bottleneck may be in supply is the servicing of land. This is a civil engineering and building problem that simply takes time and resources to solve. There is no shortage of land, but there is a shortage of serviced land. Once land is re-zoned, it is just a matter of time for it to be 'fitted out' with the appropriate services. This may seem simplistic, but if most other cities in the world can do it, then we must also be able to do it.

The next myth is that emigration has ceased, immigration has boomed and the population is soaring. There is no way to ascertain the population of the country accurately until we conduct another census and, yes, many people are coming to the country, and specifically the capital. There is, however, evi-dence that emigration has not ceased. Look for example at the figures of visas sought from the Australian embassy. Last year the number of young Irish people granted a one year work/holiday visas was 7,570. This is up from 939 in 1991/92. The number is so high that it exceeded our quota and the embassy in Dublin had to 'borrow' from the Dutch quota. These visas are not net emigration to Australia, but they are the seeds of it. A close friend of mine went for the year, came back and then emigrated permanently.

It is easy to hear a story and assume it is true because it 'kind of fits in' with what you expect. Emigration falling because we are more prosperous sounds realistic, but I could equally make an argument that more young people can travel abroad because of our prosperity. It can equally be argued that the more young people that go abroad, the more will stay abroad. It also could be said that emigrants who are returning to the country may leave again as soon as the economy slows down. The viscosity of the population movements just cannot be assumed, we have to wait for a census, and reasoned analysis by professionals.

The 'feel good' factor that permeates a real estate boom, is felt mostly by those who think they have benefited the most, this is only logical. The problem is that people who think they have benefited the most may not have benefited really, and may be acting in a way not conducive with their financial circumstances.

If you bought a house ten years ago in Dublin for £50,000, and you now estimate it is worth £150,000, then you are certainly feeling wealthy. You may figure that you only owe £25,000 on the house so your net worth is £125,000. That may be so on paper, but it means very little in reality unless you can actually realise that gain in cash. Unless you can sell your house for the £150,000, then it might as well be worth £1 million. It is an old axiom of investing, that a profit is never made until you sell. Most people who own houses cannot sell them as they are living in them. In order to sell, they must have another house to move into, be willing to live in rented accommodation, or be willing to emigrate. If you have only one house, then you have to buy another in order to sell the first, and as all houses have risen with the tide, then you will find you are relatively in exactly the same position as you were before.

You could also surmise that you have made a large gain because you were so fortunate to buy ten years ago, if you had to buy now you would have to pay more a lot money for your house. Nice try, but it doesn't work like that. I could also say that you could have invested the money in Intel shares in 1987 instead of buying a house and you would now have millions in profit. Such notional profits are, for practical purposes, meaningless. Unless you can realise the gain, and put the money in a bank, then there is no gain at the present moment. This, however, does not stop people thinking they have made some fantastic capital gain and acting accordingly. The only gain you will make is when your mortgage interest payments fall, if it has fallen, then you have extra money in your pocket. This is a gain. If you do not have a mortgage then you have no real net benefit. Any perceived benefit from an increase in prices is merely an illusion that may make you feel dangerously prosperous. Unless you can realise a profit, then you have no profit.

While house prices rose due to a certain natural increase in demand and a reduction in interest rates, prices have risen further to astronomical levels based purely on the herd instinct and other psychological factors.

Not all of this frenzy can be blamed on consumers, the builders and auctioneers have kept the pot boiling too. This has been kindly facilitated by the media who keep asking them the inane question, "Are pricing going to keep rising?" Builders and others are in business to make money, not to act as financial advisors. It is in their interest to keep the hype going, I am not inferring anything illegal here, just healthy capitalism. I have heard reliable stories that some open houses were being packed with 'rent a crowds', to keep the nerves up and pressure on the real buyers.

Many people I have talked to in Dublin who are, or were, in the process of buying houses, have been in a state of panic. And panic is as contagious as the most virulent flu virus. People are literally running from auction to auction, and viewing house after house with herds of other buyers. This, of course, creates the very prices that most of them cannot afford. What is happening in Dublin is, I believe, that demand is being brought forward and consuming current supply creating ridiculous prices. I know of many people who brought their decision to buy a house forward because of fear of not getting a house, or not being able to afford one when they wanted to buy. Many friends of mine living abroad who were planning to return in a couple of years, bought houses because they felt they would not be there when they got home. All this does is to compress demand from future periods into the current period. If we presume demand is finite, it could not be infinite, then this means that demand is lowered in future time periods by the same amount it is increasing in current time periods. So demand must eventually ease strongly.

If you can imagine ten rooms, each representing a year let's call them rooms 1992 to 2002. Each room has ten people in it bidding for a supply of houses, the more bidders in each room then the higher the price will be bid for the number of houses available. Let's assume in the 1996 room, that there are a few extra people and prices go up in that auction. Rumours spread to the 1997, 1998, 1999 and 2000 rooms that prices are going up and supply is limited. Bidders then leave these rooms and enter the 1997 room. Prices go even higher. The more prices rise in the 1997 auction, then the more people come from the other rooms in the 'future', out of fear that there will not be any houses left when it comes to them, or that houses will be too expensive. This is, in the short-term, a self-fulfilling prophecy. Well, I am sure you can see the way this metaphor is progressing, and I will leave it before it gets too messy. The point is that demand drawn from future periods will affect future prices, especially if extra supply comes on-line from the large spurt of demand during period of compressed demand. An excess of demand will usually beget an excess of supply eventually.

Those who are patient and willing to wait until 2000, 2001 or 2002 will find that not only have prices fallen drastically, but that the buyer, rather than the seller, will be king. Those who will have bought at vastly inflated prices, will be stuck with their houses and removed from the equation, and so cannot re-enter the market. The only difficulty with the above demonstration is convincing many people that the vast majority of people are probably wrong with respect to house prices. Like the psychology experiment mentioned in Chapter 5, most people cannot believe that everybody else could be doing the wrong thing, so they imitate them.

I lived in London during their property boom and it is very similar to Dublin's boom (even though it has become fashionable to debunk this theory). Both situations are the result of business cycles gone awry. What impresses me is the similarity in the activity of the people, not the economic indicators. I remember people running around London desperate to buy houses just as they are now in Ireland. I talked to people in London who were in a panic to buy. They were sure they would never get their house, when they were bidding beyond all reality with money they could not afford. Banks and building societies were lending them money they should not have been. It is similar enough in this and many other ways for me to be sure it is a strong match. There are many other comparisons that can be found if people are willing to look. I have researched and read enough to convince me that, once the panic is deflated in Dublin, supply will have broken through the bottlenecks and prices will tumble. I am willing to quantify the chance of a substantial fall in the price of houses in Greater Dublin, at around 80 per cent. By substantial, I mean a fall of 40 per cent, and probably more in some cases. I am also putting my money where my mouth is by not buying myself. I am confident I will get a good bargain when prices overcompensate the other way at the bottom of the business cycle. Yes, prices in Dublin should have risen if interest rates fell and the economy improved generally, but not by the amount they have. Panic has distorted people's perceptions.

I fully understand the situation of people in Dublin who are living in the unrelenting drum beat of "house prices are rising and not coming down". This message comes from all sides and eventually they have to assume they are wrong in being cautious, because everyone else could not be wrong. Yet history proves otherwise. In London, Tokyo and Hong Kong 'everybody' did get it wrong, from the man in the street to the heads of the largest banks and building societies. Practically every single financial institution has been involved in property fiascos and some stage. Most involved lending too much money for property which was over-inflated in value. The market falls, as does the price of the property which is the security for the loan, and the loan goes bad. 'Everybody' and the 'experts' are not always right when it comes to boom times like this. People have to make up their minds independently, however difficult it may be. I am presenting contrary information to that which is in the mainstream media and, hopefully, it increases your ability to make independent decisions.

Before I finish this chapter, I wish to discuss two issues that have arisen in the property boom in Ireland and have caused much controversy. The first is gazumping, and the second is the practice of taking deposits on new houses. Both, in effect, cover the same issue, but I will separate them.

Consumer organisations have called for both of these related practices to be dealt with by new laws. Yet I contend that this would simply do a further disservice to consumers.

Gazumping is not only a terrible word, it is a fairly divisive activity. It is still, however, legal and a reflection of the free market. If a seller can extract more money prior to finally signing a contract, then so be it. Each person acts in their own self interest and if we made gazumping illegal, then we would have to make gazundering illegal as well. Gazundering is the opposite of gazumping, it occurs during the down-cycle in a property market. It is a reflection of the lack of information about other booms that nobody I talked to in Dublin ever heard of the word gazunder. Gazundering is when the buyer reduces his, or her, offer to the seller because the buyer realises how desperate the seller is because the market is falling, or because the seller is under threat of foreclosure or some equally terrible fate. Over the years, gazumping and gazundering usually help to clear the market and provide the best prices. It represents the market at work. However, in some cases, they do seem to penalise certain people. In London I knew of people gazumped on the way up as they rushed with the rest of the crowd to buy, and then the slump came and they had to sell because they could not afford the mortgage due to unemployment. They were then gazundered by aggressive and astute buyers when selling. Rash and inexperienced people are always the victims of those who can remain composed. It is extremely difficult to legislate to protect the impetuous buyer. The basis of much consumer law is *caveat emptor*, let the buyer beware. This wariness must take place at the time of purchase.

I always associated gazumping with private contract sales between two individuals, because this is where the name originated. However, in Ireland, the practice of paying a 'booking deposit' on what you thought was a fixed price for a new house and then being asked for more, is prevalent. This is essentially gazumping, but it raises some interesting side issues because consumer organisations are demanding that these 'booking deposits' be considered fully fledged contracts. My limited study of contract law a number of years ago, would indicate to me that a contract needs offer and acceptance, intention to create legal relations, and consideration. I do not believe all of these would be present for the sale of a house based on the payment of a 'booking deposit'. However, this aside, there are strong reasons why the payment of a deposit should not become a binding agreement.

If you allow the down payment of £2,000, or whatever, to secure the right to purchase a house at a fixed price, you have effectively created what is known in financial circles as a call option. A call option allows the purchase of a financial security at fixed price, at a fixed date in the future. It thus allows speculation on capital appreciation without the commitment of the total purchase price. Let us assume you pay a deposit of £2,000 (buy a call option) on a house in April and expect to pay £100,000 for it in July. However, when July comes around, the market price is £110,000. If you can force the builder to sell it you at £100,000 then you make a notional £10,000 profit on it. In fact you could sell the right to buy the house (the deposit slip) independently for cash to someone else for anything up to £8,000 and you and he will make a profit. This would encourage speculation from investors with no intention of ever buying a house. They would simply pay booking deposits (buy options) on large numbers of houses. Whereas now, an investor needs to pay £100,000 to speculate on the capital appreciation of houses, they could buy 50 deposits at £2,000 each. This would cause more short-term volatility as speculators traded options on houses back and forth with each other, as they do with wheat, oil, pork bellies and everything else imaginable. Furthermore, builders or auctioneers might stop the practice of taking deposits in an up-cycle and sell the houses by auction or some other more expensive method – the cost being passed on to the consumer.

In the down-cycle of a property boom, legally enforceable booking deposits (options) could become what are known as 'put options'. If prices fall between the time you pay a £2,000 deposit and when you go to buy, then the builder could legally force you to buy the house. If you were not under such a legal obligation, you may be able to negotiate a better price with the developer, or abandon the £2,000 for better prices elsewhere, that will net you more than your £2,000 deposit. If the builder could force you to buy at the agreed price then the deposit plays strongly to his advantage. A builder who anticipated a fall in the property market, could take 'deposits' for £2,000 from naïve buyers, or even a lot less, to entice people into making commitments he felt were to his advantage.

It may all be swings and roundabouts in the end, but turning deposits into legal contracts is now a knee-jerk reaction. Over the short-term a legally enforceable deposit could play against consumers in Ireland as much as for them. Especially since builders have had all the advantages on the way up of no legal enforceability. Making booking deposits legally enforceable just before a market starts falling, would mean that consumers would get the worst on the way up and the worst on the way down. Consumer advocates calling for such moves may, unknowingly, be playing right into the hands of builders and developers.

This all, of course, begs the question: what exactly are booking deposits? The answer is that I do not know. If the market is good, then the builder will simply raise the price, you can pay the new price if you wish, and if you do not want to, then you get your deposit back, and he sells elsewhere. In bad times, the builder might try to force you to close the contract, but considering recent legal precedent they wouldn't have a leg to stand on. Economically speaking, booking deposits are meaningless, they simply create a small private auction situation where you have, effectively, given a deposit for the right to enter the next stage of the bidding. For the builder, they might ease cash flow slightly and simplify his selling process. Overall, they bring some order to the selling process, and separate those who are serious from those who are not.

House prices in Ireland, and Dublin specifically, are tracking the path of many a classic asset price bubble. The main reason that sparked this was because of lower interest rates forced upon us by the European Central Bank. Like all bubbles, the prices will rise with all the associated hype about never coming down, and then they will just collapse as they have so many times before. Most people of course, do not believe this, and that is essential for the boom to be maintained. For, if people did not think prices were rising forever, then they would not be buying now at the inflated prices.

9

Analogies

To know the road ahead, ask those coming back.

Chinese proverb

Analogies provide something that theory, commentary and discussion cannot. They provide solid examples from which we can draw inferences. What is important to draw from them is not any precise comparison of economic statistics, but to try to catch the general flavour and mood of the populations during these booms. Common patterns emerge and clearly demonstrate that what is happening in Dublin is not unique, just part of a common cycling pattern. Analogies also allow us to extrapolate forward and see the result that excessive demand and irrationality, ultimately, has on an economy.

Providing these analogies naturally gives more fodder for the those who wish to deny what is occurring in Dublin. It has already become standard practice to pooh-pooh anyone who attempts to compare our current boom with the one which was experienced in the south east of the England less that ten years ago. The nullification of historical analogies is a necessity in most booms and, as such, it becomes an almost ritualistic event of analogies made, and analogies dismissed. All I ask is that you read this chapter with an open mind and make reasonable inferences. There never will be a perfect analogy, no two events are ever the same, but common patterns exist in most things we do in life.

The four boom/bust cycles I wish to look at are:

- London;

- Boston;

- Hong Kong;

- Tokyo.

London, or to be more specific, the south east of England, is a good analogy to Dublin because I witnessed it, and so I can compare it to Dublin. It is also a good comparison because of the similarity in the rapid rise in house prices that occurred along with the economic boom. The housing boom began in the London area and spread to most of the UK.

London and the south east of England was at the peak of the boom in 1989-1990, the restaurants and bars were overflowing, jobs were everywhere to be had. The talk at most gatherings of twenty and thirty-something's was houses or apartments. "Have you got yours yet, get in quick, the prices are going up." It could never end, but it did. Within years, headlines in the papers were reading "1,000 homes a month being repossessed", unemployment was rocketing and businesses failing left, right and centre. The house market had ground to a halt, prices collapsed, it took until 1997-1998, for them to reach their old highs. This is the one consolation, everything is cyclical, if you can hang on, prices always climb back up.

In the meantime, many people suffered needlessly because they had followed others. People defaulted and ruined their credit record, or were stuck in houses they did not now want to be in. At one stage after the fall, the negative equity problem had encircled close to a million homes. That is 1 million people who paid too much for their homes, 1 million homes that auctioneers sold, building societies and banks lent money on, and solicitors drew contracts up for, that were worth a lot less than people paid for them.

There were no guarantors for these people, they could not go back to the auctioneer and say "but you told me". They could not go back to the media and say "but your headline said the boom was going to last forever". They had learnt that basic lesson of finance, *caveat emptor*. I knew one acquaintance who bought a house in Brighton, about an hour and a half from London and he commuted up every day. The house in County Carlow reminded me of his predicament which was why it attracted my attention. My acquaintance in Brighton told me one night over a drink that his biggest problem was not money, he had a fixed-rate mortgage and a civil service job so he was keeping above water. His biggest problem was regret: every day as he spent three hours commuting up and down to Brighton, he passed by houses within ten miles of London that were for sale for half of what he paid to buy his house in Brighton. Every day he was constantly reminded that he had borrowed an extra £60,000 for the privilege of commuting for three hours, and he could not get out of the situation. In order to buy the cheaper homes, he had to sell his house Brighton, and everything had gone down with the tide. He could only sell it for half of what he paid for it, and, of course, this would not be anywhere near enough to pay the outstanding mortgage. A classic negative equity trap.

Negative equity literally means what it says, the amount you owe on your home exceeds the amount you can sell it for. I, or nobody else, could offer any advice to this man, except to ride out the storm. The storm lasted seven years for him. The look on his face was one of the reasons I wrote this book. If there is a chance of this happening in Dublin, then people should be warned in advance. Such was the fear of negative equity throughout England in the early 1990s, after the house price collapse, that The Halifax, one of the largest building societies in the UK, offered a 'negative equity proof' mortgage. Within certain conditions, the building society agreed to buy back your house if you could not sell it on the open market for more than what was remaining on your loan. This removed the fears of first-time buyers who had seen the devastation caused by negative equity on their older siblings and friends. I doubt any financial institution in Ireland is offering such a product at the moment, although they may have to in a couple of years.

A report issued by the centre for housing research and urban studies after the house price collapse in the UK, stated that:

> The boom of 1987-1989 was underpinned by a combination of several factors. Most significant of these was the deregulation of the financial institutions from the mid-1980s, which ended the quantity-rationing of mortgages and allowed banks to compete equally with building societies which led to a rapid increase in the volume of loans, doubling between 1980 and 1990, and growing availability of high proportion mortgages (up to 100 per cent), and high loan to income ratios. At the same time there was a strong growth in incomes, itself a driving force behind increased demand for home ownership, and tax cuts were simultaneously increasing personal disposable income and expenditure.

It all sounds so familiar, yet there were differences too. The essential point is that millions of people including auctioneers, economists, bankers, and politicians, believed it was going to last, and so did I. I looked around me and figured it could never end, I could not figure out how everyone else could be wrong. It was my first lesson in finance, don't do something because everyone else is doing it, because, quite often, they are doing it because you and others are.

The comparison between Dublin and Boston was highlighted by David McWilliams, the economist who coined the 'Celtic Tiger' phrase. Mr McWilliams does not live in Ireland permanently and got the same feeling I did when he was walking around Dublin, except that he saw comparisons to Boston where he worked as a student.

He saw the same frenzied economy in Boston as he sees now in Dublin. The overflowing cafes and bars, the abundance of jobs and the shortage of flats. The booming house prices, the high technology inflow. He, however, sees much deeper comparisons between the two, because of how we have been forced to adopt interest rates unsuitable for us. Boston, and the whole New England area in the US, was growing much faster than the rest of the country but could do nothing to alter its interest rates to control this, because it was, naturally, tied into the US and used the dollar like every other part of the country. Ireland, on the other hand is voluntarily adopting an interest rate policy which is unsuitable for it. The state of Massachusetts was used as an example by many politicians as an economic miracle, and many predicted growth for years to come. Then something nobody expected happened, the Cold War ended. Many hi-tech defence dollars were removed from the economy, and the cycle began to turn. A small change in fortunes for a small number of businesses and consumers cascaded down. Spending cuts led to job cuts, which led to spending cuts and so on. From the peak of 1987 house prices fell 50 per cent and many businesses went under.

What happened in the state of Massachusetts could be a blueprint for Ireland. Ireland is a small, open economy that prides itself on being a hi-tech centre for the rest of Europe. We are however, being forced to use an interest rate set for much slower economies. House prices have risen, as has the general level of euphoria amongst the population. New cars, new restaurants, new hotels, new everything. Yet one small exogenous shock could tip us over and, the more we extend ourselves, the smaller than shock has to be. This is the problem with 'experts' telling you that it is plain sailing, no one can predict the future. There is always some small nasty surprise waiting around the corner. As the excessive optimism builds up, people forget this and assume that nothing can go wrong, because nothing has gone wrong so far. Such irrational exuberance leads to irrational pricing in such things as property. It also leads to consumers and businesses borrowing too much money.

Hong Kong was one of the Asian Tiger economies that soared too high. Hong Kong, although it is halfway around the world, is not the quintessential Asian state. It was a British colony until a couple of years ago and, as such, has a strange mix of cultures. The famous red Route Master buses trundle around the streets and many people speak English before Chinese. It was, and still is, seen as a global financial and trading centre. This, however, did not insulate it from the turmoil in Asia. Where the fund-managers and other 'experts' once saw it as a shining star, it has now lost some of its tarnish and it is being avoided. In 1997, real GDP growth was at around 5 per cent, a year later real GDP 'growth' was -4 per cent, a contraction in the economy. That is a shift over two years of 9 per cent in growth figures. Hong Kong had a real estate boom and this too has collapsed rapidly with many families caught high and dry. Unemployment is at a fifteen year high and the Hang Seng stock index is a long way from the highs it was setting a couple of years ago. Political Economic and Risk Consultancy Ltd stated:

> When times are good, it is easy to talk confidently about the future, the wisdom of certain policies and the potential to develop into a centre for one thing or another. When times are bad, however, is when the real test of a system's durability and longer term direction takes place.

Hong Kong, and most of Asia, will recover as London and Boston did, it takes time but everything recovers in the end. In a couple of years, Asia will be on track for recovery and growth. For those readers who think I am a doom and gloom merchant, I am extremely bullish on Hong Kong and the rest of Asia. Shares are cheap and so is property – if you wanted to invest in this region, now is probably the best time. This is the essence of the contrarian investment theory. The only time to invest in a region or buy property is at the point of maximum pessimism, and the only time to sell, is at the point of maximum optimism. Contrarian investment theory sits well with some of the excesses of the business cycles. When the boom is in full flight, then expectations are at their maximum, and these expectations are 'priced into' prices. In simpler language, every single optimistic event and occurrence has to occur for the price to be justified and worthwhile. It is human nature to be over optimistic in good times, and human nature to be over pessimistic in bad times. So when the economy is on the floor, and everyone is pessimistic then prices are usually driven down, unrealistically, by pessimism in the market and the media.

The important point in all phases of the economic cycle, is to rely on independent data from a variety of sources, and common sense. Information from people trying to sell you something has got to be considered suspect, yet frequently in the Irish media there are auctioneers and stockbrokers being asked about the Irish housing market or the economy. I am not denigrating either of these professions, but they are in the business of selling. Most people do not exclusively rely upon a salesman's pitch when he is selling you a car. We all expect salesmen to amplify the positive and gloss over the negative, it is their job. Similarly with auctioneers, I have not seen one single auctioneer say in public that he believes house prices will fall. It is, after all, the seller who pays an auctioneer not the buyer, and auctioneers are paid by commission. The more they sell a property for, the happier their client is, and the more money they make. Which is exactly the way it should be in our system, but take everything they say with a pinch of salt.

So from where should consumers get information? Well for a start, buying this book was a large step, not because I claim it is the sole fountain of knowledge, but because it represents a contrary position to the majority. Getting both sides of an argument allows people to make a more balanced assessment of the situation. Ireland suffers from a slight drought of symmetry in its discussion of our economy. This occurs for two reasons. The first of these reasons is that we are a very small country, and we have slightly overestimated our own importance. Many financial papers and periodicals just could not be bothered to spend too much time analysing or discussing us. The second reason why the balance of information is tilted in Ireland, is that when contrary (read doom and gloom) opinions are put forward they are simply ignored. *The Financial Times* stated very straightforwardly in a major article on EMU that due to our current monetary policy, the Irish economy was heading towards the cliff's edge, and accelerating for fear it would not get there fast enough (that is a near verbatim quotation). No one ever took much interest in that article. However, if the article had been positive, I am sure it would have been used as support for the 'Celtic Tiger' theory. Such bias is worrying. In another example, EU officials very diplomatically suggested that some prudent fiscal restraint on public pay might be wise in the 1998 budget. SIPTU reacted strongly against such advice. One almost gets the impression that they want their piece of the pie, no matter what the consequences. This again stresses the point that an economy is made up of many individuals and vocal groups that are all acting in their own self-interest. On the way up, we are all stroking in time in what looks like harmony, but once the turn in the cycle occurs, everyone will be running for cover.

I held over the discussion of Tokyo until last, as the Tokyo boom demonstrates some important points about the boom and bust phases of the business cycle. It also leads into the next chapter. Tokyo had a big boom in real estate, shares, and general economic growth, reaching a pinnacle between 1988 and 1990. The slump came in the early-1990s, but it is the reaction to that slump that is worth looking at briefly, and the impact this reaction is only now having on the rest of the world (which I will discuss in the next chapter.)

When asset prices fall after a strong, sustained rise, then banks are sometimes caught with their proverbial pants down. In many cases, they had loaned large amounts of money to investors to buy property and shares, in some cases the banks may have even bought these assets themselves. The critical function here for the banks is realistic accounting, if a loan has gone bad and the security is not worth nearly what the outstanding loan is, then reflect this in your accounts. Many banks in Tokyo did not do this after the crash, and are still not doing this. In the UK when property prices fell and the financial institutions repossessed property, then they immediately sold it and wrote off the loss. They knew they were not in the property business, they were in the money business. They took the bitter medicine and got on with things.

Banks in Tokyo today are carrying assets on their balance sheets that are not worth a small fraction of what they claim. This has caused major headaches in the economy. The system of government and financial regulation in Japan is a mess of cronyism and face-saving exercises. The problem with the Japanese banks is so big that the government is really afraid to play hardball and force the banks into full public disclosure. Their remedy to date, is to offer the banks money to cover some of the losses if they will admit these losses. Even that has not been enough to bring forward many of the sinners, they still prefer to carry on, rather than admit problems. Many of Japan's banks are, probably, technically insolvent by Western standards, the big question, and problem, is that nobody is exactly sure which ones. The fears are that possibly this problem extends to some of the industrial giants as well, who are incestuously tied to some banks. Even though Japan is a wealthy country, it has many hidden problems in its financial and industrial conglomerates.

Japan's consumers are so nervous about the future that they are just not spending money. This has exacerbated, some would say caused, the crisis in Asia. This Asian crisis could cause global problems if it affects the US and Germany seriously. If it affects these countries, then Ireland will feel the chill, and this could be the shock that tips us over.

10

The State of the World

*Do you not know, my son, with what little
understanding the world is ruled?*

Pope Julius III

This chapter marks a turn in the book, by refocusing on the future. Nothing can be done about recent history, and Ireland is where it is. The next stage is to assess how matters can develop over the next couple of years, and to consider what actions people can take. The function of this chapter is to give a brief analysis of the state of the world. Ireland is a small, open economy that could be susceptible to many exogenous shocks. The four different regions I wish to look at are:

* Asia;

* the USA;

* Europe;

* the UK.

I finished the last chapter with Japan, commenting on the reluctance of Japanese consumers to begin spending, and it is in part this reluctance, that could perpetuate the problems currently felt in Asia. However, it is not easy to claim that Japan caused the problems in Asia. The Asian 'Tigers' had extremely impressive records. Throughout the 1990s, half the world's growth came from Asia, and two-thirds of the world's capital investment went into the region. Korea was the 11th largest economy in the world and had 8 per cent growth. Thailand was the fastest growing economy in the world between 1985 and 1994. Education was reaching further into the community, and social and democratic progress were accelerating, so what went wrong? Whatever went wrong, nobody saw it coming. One International Monetary Fund annual report, for example, said of Korea: "Directors welcomed

Korea's continued impressive macro-economic performance", it praised the authorities for their enviable fiscal record. Three months later, Korea was in serious financial trouble. If IMF directors cannot see trouble the size of a truck coming, what hope does anyone else have?

The very short-term problem with most Asian economies was one similar to that experienced by some of the first banks I talked about in Chapter 1. The short-term debt exceeded the foreign exchange reserves in many Asian countries. Each investor in turn suddenly realised that if all the others took their money out, then there would be none left for him. This led to a classic run for the door, and the resulting collapse of many Asian currencies. This financial reaction was not justified considering the problems, which were serious but not dire. Panics are never subtle however. If you build up a house of cards, then someone will always come and start shaking the table. The more investors looked at Asia, the more panicky they became. One by one from 1995/1996 stock markets and property markets began to fall. Even the 'solid' countries, such as Taiwan, Korea, and Hong Kong, were impacted.

For all of the talk about 'Tigers', Asia had some fundamental problems, which it was having difficulty overcoming. Its infrastructure was congested and obstructing growth, there were critical shortages of skilled people, and there was widespread corruption in many countries. The result is that some countries in Asia have gone from having impressive growth figures to worrying about social unrest and food shortages. Banks are now nervous of lending to most Asian countries, many large Asian companies cannot even get trade credits, not to mention long-term loans.

The credit crunch from a bank's point of view is understandable, but it is going to do nothing to pull Asia out of its dilemma. The IMF is left to try to shore up matters but they have limited resources. Restoring confidence is gong to take time, but it will come eventually. Asia has great potential and this sudden downturn will probably be viewed with hindsight as a bump in the road, even if it is a very big bump. This does not, however, allow us to ignore the short to medium-term problems that the big slump in Asia presents to world commerce. Combined with this, is a growing feeling of resentment towards the US. Many Asians are now beginning to speculate that all of this was engineered in some vast conspiracy to stunt their growing economic power. However illogical this may seem, it is nevertheless gaining credence as a theory.

What has all this to do with Ireland? I have heard some say that it has very little to do with us, because Ireland has minuscule amounts of trade with the affected countries. This is naïve in the extreme; we may have very little trade with some Asian countries, but our major trading partners have extensive links, and our trading partners' problems will be our problems very soon.

The USA is currently a powerhouse of industrial might. It has shaken off the days of the 1970s and early 1980s when self-doubt crept into its philosophy. There was much talk of the flaws with American capitalism, and much fascination with Japanese and Eastern management techniques in general. These were almost raised to the status of religion by some management gurus. Now we are beginning to realise that much of the Japanese management technique involves sweeping problems under the carpet.

Most American companies simply got down to the difficult task of restructuring and embracing new technology. And it worked very well. The US is steaming along with Alan Greenspan, the head of the federal reserve, at the helm. President Clinton has maintained his popularity because of the strength of the economy. However, if truth be known, Alan Greenspan is the man who has probably created, and definitely maintained, much of the economic success experienced by the US with prudent central banking. He knows when to give the bitter medicine and when to give the pep pills.

America, however, still has some problems on its hands, as it is the only super power around. Besides the role of globo-cop, it is now expected to be globo-banker. It pulled Mexico out of the fire in 1995 and has been, directly or indirectly, involved in numerous other rescue missions. It has been prodding Japan to reform its economy, and especially the worrying banking system, for quite a few years. It has been propping up Yeltsin, some would say physically as well as metaphorically. It is now called into action in Asia. There has to be a limit as to how much it can afford to do without the strain showing.

The US economy is inward looking, in that a large majority of its trade is within its own borders, but there is enough external trade to cause significant worries. If large, American companies cannot sell their products to Asia, then this is going to impact their profits and the numbers of people they can employ. The US stock market stumbled badly for a time in 1998 because of this sudden realisation by investors. If US companies sell fewer goods, then most of them will make less profits, and have lower dividends.

Alan Greenspan became very worried about the potential for the Asian and Russian crises to spill into the US. He has made statements such as, "We are clearly facing a set of forces that should be dampening demand going forward to an unknown extent," and "It's pretty obvious, I think, that the outlook for 1999 for the US economy has weakened immeasurably." Mr Greenspan is not known for being unnecessarily alarmist, so these statements are sufficient warning for me that the US economy could slow down. In fact within days of the above statements, Mr Greenspan made the unusual move of cutting interest rates in the US outside the normal routine for doing so. This is about as much warning as the world is going to get. Any more public displays of concern by Mr Greenspan would be read by the markets as panic and then they would panic also, so Mr Greenspan is not going to make many more negative comments in public. We have been giving due warning. This is not to say that the American economy will definitely contract, or that American consumers will definitely cut spending heavily, but they may. Planning is about lining up potential events, working out their potential impact on you, and then deciding how likely each one is to occur, and balancing these figures when deciding on action.

If we have decided that the most significant potential impact could be from the Asian slump, then we need to look at precisely how this may occur and, more importantly, the affect it could have on Ireland. The three major areas impacted in the US will be jobs, banks and the stock market.

Asia's main route out of any recession would be to export their way out of it, with their devalued currencies. This means cheap imports flooding the US. This will result in a worsening of the US trade deficit, which is already very high. Adding another $100 billion to it could easily mean a million less jobs in the US. The cascading impact of this will be big, and it will curb demand for many products. The 'feel good' factor has also encouraged US consumers to spend, the 'feel fear' factor will curb this spending. The spending that will be cut will be the luxury spending, such as foreign holidays and expensive consumer electronics, to name but two. These two areas could impact Ireland. New jobless figures in the US at the end of 1998 were quietly reaching 4-year highs.

The banks in the US, and in fact worldwide, have been hit hard by the Asian crisis. The banks lent too much money to Asian companies that are now in trouble. Debt was denominated in yen and dollars so repayments are near crippling, if not impossible, for companies earning in local Asian currencies. Banks have written off much Asian debt, and probably have another sizeable chunk that is questionable. When the banks make mistakes, then other people tend to suffer along with them. The banks are not going to lend much money to Asia, or other emerging markets, for a while, and possibly cut loans in their home countries, such as the US. If the banks start rationing credit, then expansions, and new projects might not be financed with the commensurate effect on jobs and spending.

Wall Street took a big fall last year, and since then has seesawed for some time. The question of where the US stock market goes is important because most other stock markets in the world will track it. Stock markets are quite often the quintessential boom/bust scenario. Knowledgeable investors who make gains, attract naïve investors who are attracted like moths to a light. They have little understanding of the investing and are just sucked in out of greed. They know all the words, they know all the expressions, they think they can take the bumps, but they cannot. Investing in the stock market is a way to make a good return over ten or, ideally, twenty years. In the short-term, new investors will probably lose money because they are attracted for the wrong reasons. Eventually, all of the short-term investors panic and run for the door, driving the market to the floor. If this occurs in the US, then many new investors are going to lose money and stop spending to recoup it. Close to 50 per cent of the American population is in the stock market in one way or the other, and many of these are nervous new investors.

Having a nervous stock market, with everyone having one eye on the door and the other eye on everyone else, is tense enough. If you add to this the Asian crisis and possible effects on US companies, then things look very shaky. Hopefully the recent fall has cleared the market of the most nervous investors, but it is very hard to know what will happen. It is, however, something to watch, if the Dow Jones is anywhere on the wrong side of 7500 when you are reading this, then I would be concerned.

Overall it can be said that the American economy could turn down slightly, or even more severely, in 1999. It is extremely difficult to figure out what impact this will have on the Irish economy, but it could be substantial if American companies decide to jettison some plants. The idea that factories are somehow secure just because they are extremely large operations and that so much money has been invested to date, is, unfortunately, not a solid one. You only have to witness the Siemens semi-conductor plant that was built in the UK. Close to £1 billion was spent constructing it, and it was shut just after it opened its doors. Companies make decisions very rationally and they understand the accounting term of 'sunk cost'. If money has been spent, then so be it, but it should not encourage us to lose more money. American companies are extremely efficient, some would say ruthless, costcutters. They survive by cutting costs to the bone in a downturn. If plants need to go then, they will go, and go fast. However, I am fairly confident that many Irish operations are viable even in a downturn, but who knows? Many other countries are emerging, even within the EU, that can offer equally skilled staff and lower labour costs. The wisdom of our politicians boasting that our standard of living is rising to EU levels is questionable. The very reason many firms are here in Ireland is because we were below EU levels. They might do well to keep their mouths closed for a while.

The larger issue concerning a slowdown in the US economy is whether it will affect the EU as a whole and create a global slowdown as some commentators predict. Ireland could not survive being squeezed by slowing demand from the US, the UK and our other EU partners. It is clearly very difficult to tell which way mainland Europe is going to go in 1999, estimates for growth have been revised down. The most important countries from Ireland's point of view, are the UK and Germany.

The UK has growth predictions of around 1 per cent for 1999. Over the last couple of years, it applied the brakes strongly to the economy by raising rates – which is exactly what we should have been doing. The UK government saw that the economy was beginning to grow too fast and rather than risk another boom/bust scenario, it preferred to slow the economy down. What many people do not realise, is that controlling the growth rate is more important than lowering employment to levels which are too low. There is what is known as the full employment rate of unemployment. There is a certain level of unemployment that naturally exists in an economy and lowering unemployment below this causes wage pressure. In Ireland's case, there is ample unemployment to be absorbed, so general wage inflation has not occurred yet.

Overall, even though the UK economy is sluggish, it should not go into recession, unless of course, any global slump pushes it into one. Even though the economy in the UK is not burning bright like ours, their situation is much more preferable. Stable growth, even low stable growth, is preferable to our uncontrollable growth. Furthermore, the UK has had bitter experience of the hangover that can be caused by excessive growth and it is never going to make the same mistake twice.

I believe that if it was not for EMU, we would have tracked the recent interest rate path in the UK, which was a sharp rise to quell a potential boom, and then an easing when the job is done.

Which way Germany will go is anybody's guess. It is extremely difficult to predict what will happen with them. Germany has just elected a new left of centre government, with a Tony Blair look-a-like as Chancellor. Herr Schroeder, unfortunately, may not be the real power in Germany, he was just pushed to the front because he was the most presentable of his party. Oscar Lafontaine is the head of Mr Schroeder's party, the SDP, and as such may be calling the shots. He is a typical left wing German politician, who sees more regulation, more spending, and more controls as the solution to Germany's problems. Mr Schroeder has much more sensible ideas, but we will have to wait and see which of these men prevail in the end. The idea of having two leaders has rarely worked in practice, and I doubt it will work in Germany – one will have to take a back seat. But which one will it be?

This represents the state of the world as I see it when this book is being written. It is reasonable to infer that world economies are going to slow down due to the Asian crisis. Ireland is not an island in terms of trade, although some seem to think we can survive no matter what. Domestic demand simply cannot compensate for external demand for our products. We must export in order to survive. If our largest trading partners are slowing down then we can only assume our exports to them will slow as well.

A good question is: can a 'soft landing' be achieved in Ireland if our trading partners experience a slow down? Growth in Ireland in 1998 was over 11 per cent, this is breakneck speed and I cannot see how we can land gently. The reason is that it is not possible to slow down an economy as you would a car. A mere stabilisation of one sector of the economy can lead to a dramatic crash in another, which itself can precipitate an overall decline by avalanche. Let's look at a very simple, unrealistic but illustrative, example.

Assume there are 1,000 cups of coffee per day sold in Dublin every year, and this is supplied by 100 coffee machines; not much increase or decrease has occurred over the last few years. Every year, 10 per cent of coffee machines need replacement because they wear out, which represents demand for 10 machines. However, in the boom, coffee sales have increased to 1,200 cups per day. This has led to the demand for 20 new machines by the new coffee houses supplying the extra 200 cups. Business is now up from 10 to 30 coffee-making machines for the year, a relative increase of 200 per cent in demand. The coffee-machine industry expands accordingly. However the year afterwards, sales of coffee drop to 1,100 cups per day, which is a small relative fall, but it means that only 11 machines will be required as replacements for current stock with no new demand (in fact, the coffee machine market may be flooded by unused machines and cause zero sales; I will however assume this does not occur.) A fall from 30 to 11 machines is a fall of 63 per cent since the peak of last year, which resulted from a fall of only 8 per cent in actual coffee sales. If the coffee machine company had geared up production and/or sales teams, then these would have to be let go.

This is an extremely simplified, and unlikely example, but it demonstrates the geared effect that sudden increase in demand can have on certain industries, and the sharp drop that can occur when sales moderate just slightly. For the Irish economy, a slight dip in demand for certain products or services, could cause a severe reduction in associated industries which have expanded too optimistically.

11

European Monetary Union

Never assume the obvious is true.

William Safire

European Monetary Union (EMU) is the most important issue in this book, and it deserves some closer attention at this juncture. Not only has it created the current economic climate, but the whole transition to the euro is going to impact the economic future of Ireland. Not only will it cost vast amounts of resources, but there is a chance EMU will fail. Such a failure would cause an immediate and severe recession in Ireland.

We are in our current economic condition, whether you see it as good or bad, because of the immediate impact of a reduction of interest rates necessary for EMU membership. As I have contended throughout this book, I believe the lowering of interest rates will be seen in the medium to long-term as extremely detrimental. This raises the next question: are the lower interest rates, and the disruption of what could have been a normal business cycle, worth it for EMU? I think not. I not only think that Ireland's entry into EMU is premature, but that the whole of EMU is an untested proposition, from an organisation with a very bad track record. The three areas I will look at in this chapter are:

- the benefits/costs of EMU;

- the flaws with EMU;

- why we should have followed the UK's position on EMU.

Much information, some would say propaganda, has been issued from various government departments to justify our entry into EMU, and to 'educate' us on how wonderful life in euro-land will be. Most of these arguments from our own government are questionable, although on the surface they seem plausible. The supposed benefits Ireland will receive from EMU are repeated endlessly, and they are:

- lower transaction costs for consumers and business;
- price transparency;
- a common currency will create a single market;
- Irish trade with Europe will be boosted.

The EU has stated that it expects savings will be made because of lower transaction costs and reduced costs of financial hedging. This will, I am quite sure, be the case for the rest of Europe. A German may deal in francs, lira, and guilders on a frequent basis: but we are not Germans. In Ireland, the majority of our import trade and travel, is with the UK and the USA. We are simply going to be changing from exchanging punts for sterling and dollars to exchanging euros for sterling and dollars. However, there will be some gain when we are dealing with mainland Europe in foreign transaction costs, and this is a certainty. This small benefit, however, may not even be realised.

What many people seem to forget, is that it is the banks who 'impose' foreign transaction costs and so they stand to lose if, and when, these costs go. Banks need to earn a certain return on capital, and if there is a reduction in their income in one area, then they will compensate in another area. Banks are in business to earn money, and it is simplistic to think that they will absorb a loss in revenue. They will just hike cost elsewhere. If they do not, then they will have to shed staff or close branches. Banks are not charities, they are in business to earn money to pay dividends to shareholders. You should soon expect to see banks charging most customers some form of maintenance fee for just keeping an account open. They have to raise revenue or cut costs. It is all swings and roundabouts.

The next argument that our government repeats constantly is the lovely expression 'price transparency'. Price transparency will be the ability of people to clearly see the price differentials across the euro-zone because of the use of the single currency. The inferences from the government is that manufacturers are somehow involved in a Europe-wide conspiracy to defraud consumers and businesses, and a common currency will expose their practices. Yes, there will definitely be some benefits of price transparency across Europe. However, in the Irish case, our government putting forward this argument is the height of hypocrisy, as it is our government that creates most price differentials in the first place, not some cabal of manufacturers. It is our government who employs thousands of civil servants to devise and impose numerous taxes which distort prices. Are we now to assume that on 1 January 2002, when euro pricing is supposed to become Europe-wide, that our government is going to remove the huge taxes that distort the prices we pay. Let's assume I was 'mathematically challenged', and I could not figure out that a car is 30 per cent cheaper in Amsterdam than in Dublin prior to 2002, because I could not convert guilders to punts. Once this realisation is obvious to me, will our government be removing these taxes? I would like to know the exact list of products which our government thinks manufacturers are defrauding us with? Will the government allow me to order large quantities of cigarettes from a tobacco mail order firm in Luxembourg for £1.50 a packet, without interfering? Of course they won't! Yet the Maastricht Treaty states that I have the right to do so, and with euro pricing, I will now realise that £1.50 is less than £3.00.

Our government's tax base relies on the ability to separate us from the rest of Europe and tax us accordingly. It is more addicted to alcohol duties, car duties, tobacco taxes than some of those who use these products. It will continue to create these differentials whether we are using euros, pounds or Venezuelan bolivars. In fact, the one limited opportunity for most citizens to exploit a few of these differentials was with duty free sales, but this is being removed by the EU. Duty free sales subsidised travel between Ireland and the UK, and the UK and France, and some other routes. The removal of this will raise prices for everyone, which will mean fewer people will travel to other EU countries, So much for European integration. There will be, of course, one exception to the abolition of duty free allowances. Members of the European Parliament, have exempted themselves. I cannot remember who said it, but it is very apt in this case, "There is a special place reserved in hell for hypocrites."

The notion that business people are sitting around waiting for the euro to arrive before they can begin to exploit price differentials is equally foolish. A businessperson with common sense, can work out that 100FF a ton is less that 100DM a ton. If the figures are any more complicated, then most of us have something called a calculator which will illustrate any price differences. Arbitrage will occur with or without the euro; if it didn't, all financial markets would have ground to a halt many years ago.

The argument that a common currency will create a single market is interesting. I thought the Single Market Act, which we all voted for a decade ago, did that. A single market is an excellent idea and I am a strong supporter of it. Economies of scale can be exploited and all consumers will benefit. However, for Ireland, a single currency will not create a single market, no matter how tempting it is to assume that it will. A single market needs to be built from the bottom up, not the top down. Yes a single currency will create the playing field, but there is much more than just currency difficulties obstructing a single market. There are legions of regulations and differences that obstruct trade in Europe. These issues have been skimmed over because it is hoped that a single currency will untangle all of these Gordian knots. This is simply asking too much of a single currency. The euro cannot remove ingrained cultural biases and work practices. A single currency cannot dissolve volumes of technical regulations that are designed to frustrate the very free trade which the euro is supposed to encourage. On a simple level, a single currency cannot translate an instruction manual into ten different languages. The euro cannot do the hard work which governments are unwilling to tackle.

The argument that Irish trade will be encouraged with Europe in the new euro era, is also questionable, simply because we already have extremely healthy trade with other EU countries. Our trade has grown in leaps and bounds over the last 30 years. This demonstrates the critical point that Ireland doesn't need a common currency to help us boost trade with the EU, we simply need goods that other EU members want from us.

The argument that trade will be boosted, has now evolved to the argument that we will lose trade to other countries in the EU if we did not change to the euro. This is going from the carrot part of the argument to the stick very quickly indeed. Ireland has some of the best exporters and marketers in Europe simply because we have overcome many obstacles before us. We have dealt with the currency issue for long enough, I doubt that importers in another EU country will abandon us simply because of the euro. We either have what they want to buy or we don't. European business people also have calculators and have been using them in our favour for many years. Another small country in Europe, Denmark, is not joining EMU and it is obviously not particularly worried about it. And the Danish have much to lose, because the Danish have the one of the highest GDP per capita in Europe, at over $33,000 per capita. If the Danish are not worried about their exports, then should we be?

In order to weigh up any event, most people do a cost/benefit analysis. If, for example, you were going to buy a car, you may be undecided between diesel and petrol. You would not simply look at the advantages of diesel, you would look at the disadvantages of diesel, and the advantages of petrol as well. In the case of the euro, there are costs to joining it. Knowledge of them could help readers to avoid, or diminish, them.

The costs to Ireland are going to come from the costs of physically changing currency and the broader costs of the changeover to the euro connected with the preparedness of Irish companies.

The physical changeover to the euro, if it occurs, is going to be extremely expensive. Costs are going to be incurred by a wide range of people in a wide number of situations. Examples of these costs are:

•   commercial ventures needing to change coin equipment;

•   costs of changes to computer software;

•   psychological confusion over pricing.

The costs of changing equipment has not been explored much in the public forum, yet it should be, because it is the average consumer who will end up paying. The government is not going to pay these costs, retailers are not going to pay them, so the only people left are the consumers. Most people I have spoken to on this topic think that a few tills will need to be changed to deal with the euro, but it is not as simple as that. The equipment issue is much more complex. Firstly because there will be dual currencies in operation from 1 January 2002 to 1 July 2002[1] and, secondly, because there are more 'currency sensitive' machines than people think.

1.   Many sophisticated tills will need to be reprogrammed, and many older tills replaced, because they cannot deal with dual currencies. By law, the euro and the punt will be le-

---

1.   There is confusion over how long the dual-currency period will be. Six months was originally defined as the maximum figure. Although it is now suggested that it may be substantially less than this, no one can really know at this point in time.

gal tender for up to six months, and all vendors will be obliged to accept both.

2.   All coin operated equipment must be replaced, or physically changed, to accept the new euro. This includes telephones, vending machines, receptacles for coins in buses, ticketing machines, etc. Count how many of these machines you pass in your average day. Estimate the cost of having to alter each one, or physically replace it if it cannot be altered.

3.   During the 6-month period, the above machines will probably be changed to the euro gradually and will obviously only accept one currency at different times. Yet both currencies will be legal tender and can be legally given in payment. What will happen on buses? It is confusing enough for the driver to deal with one currency, let alone a second one. How will Telecom Éireann deal with public telephones? It will now not be sufficient to find a coin phone, you will have to find one that accepts the currency you have. How much chaos is going to ensue with bus tickets, train tickets, parking machines, vending machines, what will the cost be to the economy. Can it all be achieved in six months, where will all the technicians and engineers come from to do all the changing? The chaos of a dual coin society could not only go on for months, but for a matter of years, as various bodies find that they simply do not have the physical manpower to change all machinery over a 6-month period.

The costs, both monetary and time-related, will have to be borne by Irish consumers. Retail operations will simply pass on costs to the consumer, they have to, who else is going to bear them? Certainly not the government, they are simply passing on their orders from Brussels and there are no plans to offer subsidies for what they have initiated (even if they did it is all taxpayers' money in the end). The cost increases necessary to pay for equipment changeovers will, of course, be inflationary.

If you have software for simple bookkeeping or advanced financial transactions, then you are going to need to make changes. The most obvious is the '£' symbol, which will need to be replaced with the euro '€' symbol. Many people I have spoken to think they can continue using the pound sign, as it will be irrelevant what sign is used. This would be true if it was not for the dual-currency period between 1 January and 1 July 2002, when both punts and euros will be in circulation and you will need to be able to distinguish between the two currencies clearly. For many operations, there are going to be some extremely complex decisions to be made because of this dual-currency period. How, for example, do you keep accounts in two separate currencies, if your presently installed software can only handle one? Simple, glib answers like 'change the software' gets us nowhere. The costs associated with software changes are large, and the task can take years for large organisations. The questions are very complex and many problems will not become apparent until the process is running.

The dual-currency period will be a massive challenge to consumers and financial institutions alike, simply because there is no history to draw from, and every change you make generates little or nothing in short-term benefits. It is a complete absorption of resources with no tangible benefits. It may appear wonderful to an MEP that you can get on a plane and fly to Helsinki without changing currency. However, many families in Ireland cannot afford to fly to Helsinki and are more interested in the 365 days a year they spend in this country.

One of the most interesting aspects of the dual-currency period I found while doing research, is the aspect of physically storing money. There are approximately 100 billion notes and coins in circulation in the proposed euro-zone. In order to replace this currency over a 6-month period, the new euro currency will all have to be on hand on 31 December 2001. The question that the security industry keeps asking, and governments have not answered to date, is where this money is going to be kept, and who is going to transport it and distribute it. There are simply not enough vaults, security vehicles, secure money bags, etc. to effect distribution. Again the security industry is not keen on doubling its capital equipment for a period of a few months extra work. I can only presume that the army will be brought into service, but their vehicles do not appear to be much more secure than standard delivery lorries. This also raises the issue of crime. As euro notes will not actually be legal tender until 1 January 2002, it may, for legal reasons, only be considered to be worth the paper it is printed on up until 2002. Over the two years this money is being printed and readied for distribution, anyone who steals it could only face very minor misdemeanour prosecution. You could steal the equivalent of £1 million in notes, but they may only be worth less than £1 in actual paper. There is also the more serious question of whether counterfeiting of the money would actually be illegal. If the euro notes would not be legal tender until 2002, how could you be counterfeiting them prior to this? All of these issues might seem to be only interesting trivia, but they could jeopardise the acceptability of the currency. It takes just one judge in a court in Dublin to interpret the law, to define counterfeiting as replication of a physical 'legal tender', and if you cannot legally tender the euro notes for settlement of debts, then it cannot be legal tender. Imagine the chaos then, with open counterfeiting of the currency allowable up to midnight on the 31 December 2001. Then what? The possession of these counterfeit notes would be illegal, and the Gardai would immediately crack down on perpetrators when they find them. How is this going to mix with attempting to get an entire population to accept new notes which they have never felt or seen up close before. The government will be trying to get everyone to accept a new currency, while at the same time, the Gardai are warning them to beware of the huge amount of counterfeit notes that criminals are trying to pass. I am sure the geniuses over in Brussels are working on this one, but I see no ready solution, and who is going to suffer? It will be the old-age pensioner, the weak-sighted and the extremely trusting.

While the physical cost of changing over is going to be substantial, there are also going to be psychological issues. From the date widespread pricing begins in euros, 1 January 2002, everyone is effectively going to be living in a foreign country. Most consumers operate on price points for evaluation purposes, and these will be distorted. We all gauge prices by comparing them to known goods. If you see a new product for £1.50, you know which other products cost around the same and can gauge the amount of utility you derive from that product, and so you can make a reasonably informed purchasing decision. A change in currencies will mean that this system will be undermined and prices will have to be re-learned. For those of us young enough to do so, that may be an acceptable cost, but I know many older people who never changed with the 'modern money', i.e. decimalization. I vaguely remember the changeover as I was only a very young child, but for a long time after, my grandmother never got to grips with the new currency. In fact, even now in her eighties, she still sometimes talks in 'old money'. Change is quite often difficult, and while this should not be a reason to avoid it, it is a factor to be taken into consideration.

There are some oddities about Ireland's conversion to the euro that will only affect us. The euro will be worth approximately 75 pence, this means that we are the only country whose unit of currency is worth more than the euro, and also whose currency value is roughly similar to the euro. In Italy, for example, the shift in prices will be instantaneously noticeable because of the sizeable scale difference. In Ireland, the price changes are going to be close enough to cause confusion, and wide enough to appear inflationary. If we look at an example of a product that sold for £1.10, it will sell for approximately €1.46 after the conversion. This will give a general, and repeated, sense of inflation to many consumers. Furthermore, many people will be unsure as to whether prices will be accurately calculated, or whether the retailer is adding on a few extra cents to recover equipment costs, or just to make a quick buck in the confusion. RTÉ should be able to programme an entire hour of broadcasting every day for a year around the complaints from consumers about exploitation.

The EU in its infinite wisdom, is mandating that all prices, for a fixed period of time, will be displayed in both currencies/prices. It is not clear whether this will be on the products or just displayed at some central point. More than likely, retailers will just have a conversion chart displayed at some point in their stores. In fact, putting two prices on each item would actually be confusing in the Irish case because the euro sign and the pound sign look roughly similar, and if you put both those prices on an item it will only lead to more confusion.

It is rather strange logic to me, that, in order to obtain price transparency with countries such as Finland and Portugal, Ireland has to be plunged into price opaqueness for years. When consumers become disorientated over prices, this may lead to postponement of purchasing decisions or misallocation of money. A 'misallocation of money' may be an acceptable cost for a relatively prosperous person who mistakenly spends too much on something, but it could be a serious mistake for a pensioner who misallocated their pension and ends up short of money to buy essentials before pension day. It is always the weakest in our society who suffer in time of change. A postponement of purchasing decisions could occur if people simply become confused between comparisons. For a number of months, or possibly longer, there will be two currencies in circulation, two prices, and, consequently, ample confusion. Consumers buying certain items may simply become confused in the fog of figures facing them, and postpone a purchasing decision until they can recalibrate. There are many items people do not need urgently and might defer buying, and this could upset the natural flow of spending in commercial transitions.

There is one final cost I foresee for consumers. This is in the area where prices are set at some psychological pricing level, or where the commodity is delivered in some fixed unalterable quantity. This is an area where prices could rise with no extra gain. This will happen because of the natural tendency to round prices to .05 or higher increments. Prices involving 'copper' are rare for many items, in fact some prices are currently at £1.00 simply because of the convenience of this price.

If you pay £1.00 now for a bus or train fare, this will become €1.33 in 2002. That price will not be acceptable because of the high 'time cost' of dealing with €1.33. One coin representing a pound can be handed in precisely and dealt with quickly. The new euro price becomes as awkward as J Alfred Prufrock's romantic endeavours. €1.33 would need five coins at best, a €1 coin, a 20 cent coin, a 10 cent coin, one 2 cent coin and a 1 cent coin. This increases the awkwardness and friction of the transaction. In order to smooth this transaction somewhat, the price will probably go up to €1.35, and possibly even €1.40. This is still a messy amount of coins but the sum will be easier to deal with and avoid the use of small 1 cent pieces. Even the small rise to €1.35 represents a 1.5 per cent rise and will add further to inflationary pressure, as you cannot add utility to a simple journey from point A to point B. Another item that will be affected this way are newspapers, *The Irish Times* will change from £0.85 pence to approximately €1.08. The natural inclination will be to raise the price to €1.10 to smooth the transaction out. The contrary argument will be that some prices close to an even price point will be falling to balance this out. However, we all know exactly what will happen – every price will rise and none will fall.

These are all complex, and sometimes subtle, problems that no politician wants to talk about, yet they will have to be faced, as they are a real cost of converting to the euro – a path which we have been set upon without much consultation. We were told that if we did not sign the Maastricht Treaty, that we would be ejected from Europe. On the sweetener side, we were told we would get £6 billion. I wonder whether we ever got the £6 billion and what was done with it.

All of the arguments that we should join have now been reduced to, "Well, we are committed now, there is no turning back." This may be so, but it is not a very sophisticated argument for changing our currency unnecessarily and handing sovereign control of our monetary policy to another government. Denmark, which exists on the fringe of a huge EU partner, not only rejected the Maastricht Treaty, but received the concession of being able to opt out of the common currency for doing so. The Danes are not worried about any of the catastrophic woes that would befall them, mostly because they know they will not happen. The only justification I can find for why our government did not negotiate an opt out from EMU for us, was because of the £6 billion. It may seem like a lot of money, but it is only around £1,500 per head, not much money for our economic sovereignty.

This leads on to the broader discussion of EMU. The question of whether Ireland should be in EMU is supplanted by an even larger, as yet unanswered question: will EMU work? The expectation of most people that EMU will work, is founded on what they have been told by their governments or the EU, but it should come as no surprise that these entities sometimes count their chickens before the proverbial eggs have hatched. While it may seem like apostasy to even question EMU at this stage, I treat it like all other propositions and apply critical analysis. I personally put the chances of EMU surviving to the stage where physical currency is issued, at slightly above 50 per cent. The reasons which lead me, and many others, to be so sceptical are simple.

1.   EMU is effectively a fixed exchange rate system[2] which progresses to a common physical currency. No fixed-exchange rate system has ever endured. They have always been prised apart because, ultimately, the nationalistic interests superseded the greater good of the broader body. Nationalism is still rampant in the EU, every state politician fights for the benefit of his home country. There is nothing inherently wrong with this, but it demonstrates that, when

---

2.   I realise there are many differences between EMU and a fixed exchange rate system, but, on one level, it is a fixed-rate system and not a common currency until we are all using the euro.

push comes to shove, nationalism nearly always wins out. Professor Brendan Walshe stated recently that, "History suggests fixed exchange rates between sovereign governments do not endure." He further stated that individual governments will not stand idly by and let their economies sink for the greater good of euro-land.

2.   The EU does not have a good record in the implementation of large projects, just look at the common agricultural policy. The ERM failed in 1992-1993, speculators put the crowbar into the visible nationalistic cracks and prised them open easily. Many arguments are put forward as to why ERM failed, but most are simply excuses. The ERM was originally described as the "glide path" for monetary union, and the ERM failed, so why are we proceeding with EMU? It is convenient to get the band going and give speeches about some hazy vision of a united Europe with a single currency, but practicalities must be addressed. ERM was exposed by speculators as weak, I see no strong arguments why such conditions could not occur again.

The argument is now made by EU officials, that EMU survived the currency 'turmoil' in 1998 that accompanied the Russian crisis, and, therefore, it will survive other similar turmoils. This is an interesting argument as it leads me to ask the questions, was the ECB expecting EMU to fail? What probability had been apportioned to this likelihood? And why was it not discussed in public? What kind of problems could have occurred? Why had the possibility of such problems not been highlighted before? What is the likelihood that they will occur again? This is indicative of the whole attitude surrounding EMU, in which no chance for potential trouble is ever admitted in public in case it causes a lack of confidence. Keep the public in the dark, just tell them everything will be wonderful. What are they not telling us now? Chancellor Kohl once said that the euro would succeed if we all believed in it. This kind of fragility with a new currency is worrying; what if people decide not to believe in it? Many Germans do not want it, and much prefer their Deutschmark. Speculators may not only not believe in it, they may actively conspire against it, if they believe it is a weak currency. Currency speculators are relentless and feed like sharks. Once blood is detected, they gather in a huge feeding frenzy. To give you a example of the size and power of the foreign exchange (FX) markets, the daily turnover is $10 trillion, that is ten thousand billion US dollars a day. The volume of money flowing in the FX markets is like a wind tunnel for currencies, it tests them well.

3.   The eleven countries that comprise EMU are not what could be considered an 'optimal currency area' (OCA). An OCA is an area in which a common currency could be expected to work efficiently because of social, cultural and financial similarities. The USA is an optimal currency area, as is the Republic of Ireland, as are most other sovereign countries. A currency is more than just pieces of paper, it carries with it a lot of baggage. For the euro to work efficiently inside its area, there must be certain factors at work. These would include the ability of the area as a whole to react to asymmetric shocks. If there is a boom in Texas and a recession in California, then many people and resources will move from California to Texas. Shortages in one area are usually compensated for by excesses in another. With such a geographically mobile population, the US can normally calm a boom successfully in one area while avoiding a severe recession in another area. This is simply not possible in Europe. While some professionals and students move around inside the EU-zone, there is no broad geographic mobility of labour. If there was, then there would not be the differences in recession/boom across Europe which there are at the moment. In fact, there are very strong barriers. If Ireland went into a recession in two years time, and Finland boomed, how many families would move to Finland. The first obvious barrier is language, not many people speak Finnish, and it would take about a year to learn proficient Finnish if you were so inclined. Secondly, professional qualifications in one area may not be recognised in another area. Most individual nations jealously guard their qualifications. In Germany practically every trade and profession is closely regulated. The other limiting aspect is information; how would an unemployed carpenter know of carpentry jobs in Finland without going there? And why would he go there if he didn't know there were carpentry jobs? How does the employer in Finland

know their are carpenters unemployed in Dublin. The labour office in Dublin certainly wouldn't be much help, and I doubt many people could name one single Helsinki newspaper, let alone obtain one. That is assuming you have learnt Finnish in order to read the employment pages.

All of these factors, and many more that space precludes me from talking about, lead me to conclude that the euro-zone is in fact, a less than ideal OCA. This has been glossed over in the rush to get to EMU. The hope that the euro will somehow make the eleven participating countries an OCA is wishful thinking. A currency cannot solve complex, deeply rooted social and economic regulatory issues across Europe, it can merely highlight some of them.

The discussion so far in this chapter has been based on highlighting the many problems and costs associated with the euro and the implementation of it. I question not only the viability of EMU, but the logic of whether Ireland should be involved with it. Should we possibly have followed the UK's example and sat on the sidelines?

The UK was burned badly with its experience in 1992 when it was driven out of the ERM by speculators. This was not, of course, the speculators' fault, but the fault of the British government for exposing itself to such activity. Either way, the present UK government is extremely nervous of any fixed-rate system or common currency in Europe. While Mr Blair and the Chancellor of Exchequer, Gordon Brown, wish to look euro-friendly they have not committed to join the euro, and I am quite sure they will never join the euro, unless it is strongly in their own interest. What Mr Brown and Mr Blair have been doing is playing politics. Recently, they have been setting up committees and focus groups, and 'preparing' people for the euro. This is merely a shell game, they have made no firm commitment, except to say it will not be in the lifetime of this parliament. Neither has the UK joined ERM II, which is the 2-year proving ground for EMU.

What the UK government has been doing is preparing for EMU, and if it is a success and is running well between 2002-2003 then the UK will seriously think about joining. Then the UK government must overcome another hurdle that few other governments have had to face. They will have to have a referendum on replacing sterling. The British people are very fond of sterling and many are extremely conservative at heart. I can already see the headlines in newspapers such as *The Sun* and *The Star*, "Achtung! – Hands off our cash Fritz."

Winning a referendum on joining EMU will be extremely difficult for the Blair government, or any other UK government. Which leads me to another conclusion, the real indicator that Tony Blair is serious about joining EMU will probably be when he begins publicly to question whether a referendum is really necessary.

In the meantime it will serve them well that they have been 'preparing' for it, and they currently get some political mileage in Europe by looking euro-friendly. On the other hand, if the EMU fails or falters, they will move away from the scene of the accident and not wish to get involved. This is a near perfect EMU strategy and one which we should have been pursuing all along. We should not be entering EMU unless we are sure it is going to work, and sure the UK would also be in it; why are we taking a risk that we do not have to?

The current UK government has realised, as did the Conservative government before it, the inherent differences between the European social market view of capitalism and the Anglo-Saxon view of capitalism. The UK operates, as Ireland does, a relatively lightly regulated economy where workers have adequate but not onerous protections. It is thought that the 'invisible hand' of the market will achieve the best for the majority of people. The social market view of capitalism, which is revered on the continent, attempts to regulate much that it should not be involved in.

Many Irish people view Europe through rose-coloured spectacles. I know I did, until I actually went to live in Germany. While each country has its pros and cons, and it is impossible to say one is better than the other, it is easy to say that cultural differences intertwined with the social-market view makes living in continental Europe a completely different experience to living in Ireland or the UK.

Irish people have certain in-built cultural and economic values that we find hard to change. Owning our home is one of them. The thoughts of living in rented accommodation all our lives goes strongly against our grain. Yet in most of Europe, the majority of people live in apartments all of their lives. This is completely alien to us. We acquired from the British, the desire to own our own homes. It is a primary financial goal of nearly every couple when they first get married. The Americans, Australians, and Canadians, also inherited this desire from the British. Even though we inherited it from the British, it probably represents a reaction to the 'landlord' figure. We do not like the idea of anyone owning the property in which we live. We cherish the idea that we own the four walls around us and that we can close the door on the world. "A man's home is his castle" is not just a trite expression, it is a basis for doctrine that is enshrined in our legal system. The government cannot invade our property without strong due cause. Many Europeans do not have this strong desire to own their own home, and, even if they did, the cost of housing is so prohibitive that very few can afford to own their house or even apartment. Vast amounts of wealth are owned by very few individuals throughout Europe. Europeans have a prosperous lifestyle, but really own very few tangible assets.

There are many other European traits that only become apparent once you live in a European country and many go against what Irish people would like. When we joined EMU, we handed over control of our monetary policy to the ECB in Frankfurt. We have also, I believe, effectively handed over control of our fiscal policy. Many Eurocrats are now suggesting how we should structure our budget – how long before these suggestions become demands? There are already legal controls in place to limit budget overspending by euro states, generally a good thing, but circumstances may necessitate otherwise. On a deeper level, the loss of the right to control these polices affects our lives in many other ways. Even though house prices will fall back, they may never return to early-1990s levels. The 'right' to own a house has moved up the socio-economic scale. We have given away more than we know. If suggestions were made that we hand such powers to London, there would have been uproar for obvious, historically sensitive reasons. However, our interests may now lie more with the UK, and this will become more apparent. We have strong social, cultural and economic ties with our neighbouring country. For the few differences we have with them, we have much more that binds us together, and the UK's position on EMU may yet prove to be the correct one. I am strongly pro-European, and always will support the concept of the EU, but good fences make good neighbours.

The UK is taking a very prudent position based on its experience. The government is simply saying by its actions that it is

not sure if EMU will work. It will wait and see if the euro operates efficiently and then decide to join, if this suits it economically. Our Finance Minister, in his comments about the UK, has
tried to infer that the UK position is somehow taking advantage
of other peoples actions. He said, "If the euro proves an outstanding success, those of us who went in at difficult times and
took the heat, might take a jaundiced view of others who waited
to see if it would be a success." This seems a strange view, the
UK is a sovereign government and acts in the best interests of its
citizens. How can it be blamed for not wanting to take part in
something it is concerned about? Why should the British government take chances with its economy, just so that we can feel
comfortable. Our government and the EU like to use phrases,
such as 'fast track', 'first wave', and 'two tier', to suggest that
jumping into the euro at the beginning is some great advantage
that will benefit us. The inferences are made that there are the
brave and the weak at heart, and we will gain some special rights
by going first. This is simply not so, you only have to look at
Denmark and the UK; both have opted out and not suffered for
it. The UK simply has little interest in joining the euro right now,
and this is, I believe, starting to worry our government. We always hoped, quite possibly even assumed, that the UK would
join EMU with us. Up to recently, there was talk of the UK rush-
ing in at the last minute to join. Without the UK involved in
EMU, our membership is beginning to look less logical, even illogical. I firmly believe that if our government knew that the
UK might never join EMU, that it would not have joined either.
It cannot admit this, of course, because the Irish government
cannot give the impression that we would want to track the UK's
position. Which is of course, exactly what we should have done.

Ireland's excursions into European monetary policy have been
nothing but a tangled mess. From the day we broke with sterling
in 1979, we have been adrift in a sea of exchange rates. We have
a schizophrenic policy because we have wanted to appear mon-
etarily separate from the UK (for valid reasons), but at the same
time everyone spends their time worrying about our exchange
rate with sterling. We have now stumbled into joining a monetary
union with other countries which are economically, financially,
and culturally out of phase with us. While, at the same time, our
streets are full of UK retailers eager to expand into Ireland, and
there are millions of native born Irish living in the UK. I would
love to find out how much money has been made by financial

institutions changing sterling into punts and back again. This lucrative practice for them will, of course, continue with EMU. Every single argument that can be made for us to join EMU, could have been made for a monetary union with the UK. The only obstacles were a few sensitive historical ones which carry no economic validity, and the £6 billion that was dangled in front of us. I wonder whether our passion for EMU is such that if we had to pay a billion to join the club, we would have done so.

12

Chronology of a Recession

*For every action there is an equal
and opposite reaction.*

Isaac Newton

The last two chapters have been setting the stage for this one, which is a discussion of how a downturn in the Irish economy could occur in Ireland. While I am fairly certain that a downturn must occur, it is difficult to say when and how. I do, however, present two different scenarios based on two possible down-cycles. One is bad, and the other worse. Not very encouraging news, but they are not designed to be 'feel good' stories. Their aim is to wake people up from any financial slumber which the current boom may have induced.

The final three chapters of this book demonstrate how individuals and business can assess their current financial health and attempt to make themselves 'recession proof'.

The two scenarios are based on what I believe will be the outcome from the current economic path on which we have been put. The boom we are experiencing is unsustainable, growth cannot continue on such a level. The slowing down of this growth will expose individuals and businesses that have overreached themselves. Many will be forced to engage in serious retrenchment, this retrenchment will cause more retrenchment, and many more people will be affected as the wave grows. The magnitude this wave will reach is difficult, if not impossible, to predict, however, most recessions tend to be inversely related to the euphoria and abandonment that preceded them. I see no reason why Ireland should be any different.

The one question that people tend to ask is, "When will the downturn occur?" The answer is that I do not know. It can be likened in one way to asking a meteorologist when will the summer end. It may end early, it may end late, but it will end, of that he is certain. The problem with business cycles is that they are neither precise nor regular, like the seasons, and sometimes it is only possible to see waves in hindsight. With Dublin, however, the progressive building of the upside is quite visible, that is if you are willing to call it an upside and not some historic shift in economic theory or some 'new mode'.

All of the above being said, and considering the general level of euphoria and the asset prices, it is difficult to see matters getting much hotter, yet who knows. It may be happening as you read this, it may be another year before the fall begins to accelerate noticeably. The danger of laying a fixed time on it, is that when the time arrives and nothing significant has occurred, people assume that the all clear has been given. It is not a question of if, but of when, and how severe. I keep looking for signs that consumers are slowing down or 'cashing in their chips' but I do not see it. Every day I read the Irish newspapers, I get more worried. More extravagant building plans, further special interest demands from workers, more headlines castigating the doubters and calling for full steam ahead.

In one recent article, I noticed that Mr McWilliams, the economist who coined the phrase 'Celtic Tiger', was called an "outsider". He had called the property boom in Dublin exactly what it is, a bubble, and had made some very astute comparisons between Dublin and Boston in the 1980s. It is amazing how fleeting glory was for this obviously talented economist. His words were repeated a hundred thousand times when it suited everyone to justify their excesses, but as soon as he suggests some mild caution, he is cast aside as an unbeliever. I take my hat off to him for standing up publicly and attempting to give his honest opinion in the face of such euphoria.

SCENARIO ONE

Scenario one is premised on much of what has been discussed so far in this book. Many consumers are overreaching themselves on two fronts. They are borrowing too much, and not saving or preparing for the eventuality of any small downturn. This is because their expectations have been raised to such a level that quite a number do not expect a downturn. This does not mean that all consumers are behaving irresponsibly. It is not necessary that all consumers behave recklessly, just a significant number.

Once any small downturn occurs, these reckless consumers must cut back expenditure sharply, and this in turn will affect other, more responsible, consumers.

The scenario for a small downturn is already on the cards. With the Asian crisis starting to slowly impact the US market, consumer confidence there is showing a downturn. A downturn in the US market would create a commensurate effect on the rest of the world, and Ireland would feel the impact from all of its major trading partners.

Let's assume, for this small example, that one day Ireland wakes up to the news that one of the big US plants was closing down their operations due to lack of global demand. Factories close, companies consolidate operations, markets shrink, it happens every day. It is folly to think it will not happen in Ireland if there is a global slowdown. A single closure, and loss of a thousand jobs, could be a jolt for many people. It could start making people think about their jobs, which they always assumed were secure. Yet, that factory that closed down was meant to be secure. A simple extrapolation of fact could make many consumers cautious, and awaken them to how precarious their financial position is. You look at the bills you have to pay, you think about the bills you have coming, you talk to others who so confidently boosted you, and now you sense a little concern in their voices. The best description of this sensation I have read was by Lars Tvede in his book *Business Cycles*.

> *This feeling does not normally evolve as a consequence of a single event; it is rather because of a number of incidents that somehow do not fit the bigger picture you happened to believe in ... and you realise that you have been walking on the thinnest of ice that may break at any moment. Almost panicky, you feel that you must reverse you actions instantly.*

The closure of this hypothetical factory may only put a thousand people out of work, but it will indirectly affect many others. Local shops will notice the drop in trade, local pubs and restaurants will notice a small downturn. Piece by piece, step by step, a group of people will begin the get the feeling that they are on the "thin ice" mentioned above, and slowly begin to back away. What seemed like a bargain just weeks before, will seem like an extravagance. The closure of a big 'trophy factory' will, on its own, not affect the economy severely, but it will take the edge off the boom. It is the perceptions of the consumers that matter, and it is these that must alter to start the downward slide. A large closure will sow the seeds of doubt in people's minds that all is not well. It may not even be one closure, it may simply be small, but perceptible layoffs, a reduction in overtime, less hiring, and so on. What is essential is that people's perceptions are altered from feeling prosperous, to feeling nervously prosperous or even anxious. This small movement in the scale of perceptions will mark the start of the down-cycle.

The media will start running headlines and stories just slightly ahead of the curve, that a change may be in the wind. Once this perception gathers pace, there will be no stopping the downturn, people will begin to cut back spending. The luxuries will be the first to go, one less meal out a week, one less this or that, no new car. The less spending, the less demand and less demand means fewer jobs. Restaurants and cafes will start to let one or two people go, whose spending, in turn, will be affected. In the same way that it occurred on the way up, spending affects demand, and demand affects jobs, and total income affects spending.

The housing market will turn down. Whether it will lead, or follow a general economic slowdown, is difficult to say, but I personally think it will lead it. House prices were seen as permanently going up, 'everyone' said they could not fall. Once it is accepted that house prices are falling, then people will really become worried. There will, of course, be strong resistance in accepting that prices are actually falling. It is not going to be very palatable for those people who paid ridiculous prices and were assured that they were getting a bargain or getting in before house prices moved beyond their reach. The moment that house prices turn will, in hindsight, be easy to see, but at that moment it will be very difficult simply because the near certain expectation that house prices cannot fall, will lead to a misreading of the initial turn. Not until the fall has progressed substantially, will there be widespread acceptance that the fall has occurred.

Another facet of the downturn will be the credit squeeze by the financial institutions. Some loans will begin to go bad, and the financial institutions will begin to realise that they have lent too much money to too many questionable credit risks. They will now begin to withdraw and limit credit. This is known as a 'credit squeeze', it will cause further problems for the economy as it will force people to contract their spending to pay off more debt.

The mortgages, the term loans, the overdrafts, the credit card debt with rates of 20 per cent or more, will all loom nearer on the horizon. While income was flowing strongly, it was easy to keep ahead of the train, now that income is starting to dry up, many people will feel like they are running on the tracks with the train just feet behind them. Businesses that had been operating at full steam, will begin to realise that turnover may have masked some integral problems. When cash flow begins to recede, these problems can be revealed.

The downturn, after a period of consumer euphoria, can be something like waking up after a fairly wild party. You begin to think back on what you did only last night and wonder what had possessed you, and you just hope nobody had a video camera. The problem with financial excesses is that they do not go away with a couple of aspirin. The largest headache for most people will either be unemployment, excessive debt, and possibly negative equity for the new generation of householders.

The big question is how far down will a recession go: does the economy fall back to where it was in the 1980s? I do not think it will. There will probably be a sharp contraction, but the economy will bounce back from the bottom and assume an upward course eventually. Everything is cyclical, after day there is night, and soon after again, day. This all, may take a number of years of extreme discomfort. If people are not going to learn prudence from having the government impose it on them with higher interest rates, then they are going to learn prudence from experiencing the costs of excesses imposed upon them. Some people I have spoken to are under the illusion that if things do go bad, the government will somehow bail them out. This line of thinking is dangerous; while our government provides some basic social safety nets, a government is not going to bail out consumers who acted irrationally, even if they did tacitly encourage it.

On the bright side, economies always recover. No matter how sharp the contraction is, there is always an upturn and another up-cycle. Ireland will be no different.

SCENARIO TWO

The first scenario may have seemed fairly dire, but in fact, it was the good scenario. Scenario number one, no matter how difficult, would probably be a short, sharp contraction lasting a year or two and the financial pain for many who did not overextend themselves may be limited.

The really bad scenario will occur if EMU hits problems. Everything stems from EMU, and everything may return to it. If EMU breaks up, then interest rates will revert to what they should have been 'naturally', which will be roughly what they are in the UK. This could mean a move from 3.5 per cent to 7 per cent at maximum in short-term rates, and a similar increases in other rates. This would mean an increase of between 50 per cent to 100 per cent in interest charges on most loans. We are, of course, assured that nothing could go wrong with EMU, it is an absolute certainty. I believe that EMU will probably work, but that is just a barely over 50 per cent 'probably'. I also believe that there is a good chance that some countries may break away, or be forced away, from EMU in the early years and this could cause turmoil.

If EMU breaks up, or Ireland is forced out of it, then the interest rates would be up in a matter of minutes to support the punt as a free floating currency again. The sudden rise in interest rates would be enormous and cause a severe and sharp recession almost instantly. I do not need to spend pages drawing out the picture for people, suffice to say, it would be bloody.

It may seem unlikely that EMU will break up, but it is certainly possible. Anderson Consulting, one of the most prominent consulting firms in the world, has highlighted it as one of three possible scenarios in their recent report on the various paths EMU may take. Private organisations are realistic about future events because they have to live with the consequences. The politicians and bureaucrats who have promoted EMU cannot admit, and will not even discuss, the possibility of EMU failing. Why is this? Such near certainty of success is worrying.

EMU is attempting to bring together eleven countries under one currency. Ten of these countries already have their own currencies and each of these currencies have its own history. The Deutschmark has, historically, been a strong currency and the lira a weak one. A currency is a reflection of the country that 'owns' it, the economy of that country, the Central Banks management of that currency, and the stability of the government. There are fundamental differences in many European currencies, and the governments that manage them. The euro is going to be a weighted average of all the currencies, but until the euro comes into existence, and the other currencies electronically and physically cease to exist, there may be situations when the market perceives one currency is weaker than another. If this happens, speculators will be ever ready to 'exploit' the situation.

Between the start of this year, 1999, and 1 January 2002, the national currencies will still be in circulation and will be locked together at fixed exchange rates via the euro. The euro will be technically in existence, but not physically, although it will supposedly be the only real currency in the 'euro-zone'. All national currencies will be considered sub-denominations of the euro in the same way that a £5 note is a sub-denomination of a £10 or £20 note. This is the theory, but it, unfortunately, sounds too simple. Speculation is supposed to be made impossible because the speculators cannot deal in the individual currencies. If a speculator wants to buy Deutschmarks and sell lira, he will be only buying and selling euros. This is a grave underestimation of the abilities of speculators.

I will digress for a moment for an explanation of how speculators operate. Speculators who think one currency is overvalued, or undervalued, against another currency, engage in fairly simple practices to make a profit from the fall which they anticipate. They love fixed-rate systems, which lock one currency against another, because they assume that at some stage, the artificially fixed-rate will stray away from what they would be in an open market. Governments will of course, prop up the currency and make speeches swearing that they will never break the fixed link, but many times they do.

To illustrate this, let's look at a simple example. The Hong Kong dollar is fixed to the US dollar for various historical and commercial reasons. This currency has been fixed for quite some time, but recently speculators have begun to surmise that the fixed-rate is too high. Let us for the sake of simplicity assume that the rate between HK$ and US$ is 7 to 1. That is, for every US dollar you exchange, you receive 7 Hong Kong dollars in return. Speculators who think the HK$ is weak, also realise that the Hong Kong government will probably never devalue on its own, so the market system must force it upon them. Speculators are part of that market system. Their desire is, naturally, to make a profit, not improve the market per se, but both are really the same thing if the market is out of balance. They achieve their desire to make a profit by forcing the government to buy endless amounts of its own HK$ off them. If the government thinks the currency is worth what it says it is, then let them prove it. Speculators do this by the following procedure: a trader will borrow a huge amount of Hong Kong dollars, let's say he borrows HK$70 million from a Hong Kong bank. He then immediately sells them for US dollars in the currency market; if the Hong Kong government wishes to keep the fixed exchange rate, then it will, effectively, have to enter the market to support the price and keep it at 7 to 1. The trader now has US$10 million which he sets aside in a bank account. His hope is that the government will devalue the Hong Kong dollar. Assuming that the government does not wish to keep buying its own currency with its limited supply of US dollars, will it break the fixed exchange rate system by not intervening in the market anymore, and let the free market dictate the price?

If we further assume that the Hong Kong dollar floats to 8 to 1, i.e. a devaluation because it now takes eight Hong Kong dollars to buy one US dollar (instead of seven) the dealer has US$10 million which he sells for HK$80 million, and repays his debt to the Hong Kong bank which was fixed at HK$70 million. He has made a profit of HK$10 million, which is worth US$1.25 million, a very nice profit courtesy of the fact that the Hong Kong government obstinately stuck with fixed-rates in the face of the market reality.

This was a very simple example, which is factually untrue as the Hong Kong dollar has not, at the time of writing, been 'devalued'. There are many frictions with the above scenario for the speculator; it is far from plain sailing. Firstly, he has to be sure that there will be enough money to 'break the bank'. A paltry $10 million is not enough, he will probably need billions, which will require a general consensus from other traders that the fixed-rate can be broken. Furthermore, the Hong Kong government is a tough fighter and can battle the market for quite some time. Finally, the money the speculator borrows in Hong Kong, is going to cost him large daily interest rate bills. Every day it costs him to keep his position open. The government of Hong Kong can raise interest rates to make him hurt, hoping the pain will become too much. It is all a test of nerve and skill, if those who think the currency will break lose their nerve, they have to reverse their positions, sometimes at a loss. There are also many other complicating factors, and the above demonstration was simplified, but it is basically what happens.

George Soros 'gambled' billions of dollars that sterling was overvalued against the Deutschmark, he won out, and the ERM link was broken. He made close to a billion pounds sterling on the day that Norman Lamont was forced to pull sterling out of the ERM, even after standing on the steps of the Bank of England only hours previously and vowing never to withdraw. It is a testimony to the level that these speculators will go, that Mr Soros had the videotape of this denial immediately analysed by a psychologist, who said that Mr Lamont did not believe what he was saying because he was blinking too much.

Now we shall return to the topic of EMU. EMU has theoretically eliminated the ability to trade individual currencies by creating the euro on 1 January 1999, and making all national currencies subdivisions of it. It is believed that, if speculators wish to attack one individual currency, they will be wasting their time as they will effectively only be changing £5 notes for £10 notes. This may be a little premature, because I can think of a number of ways to speculate against individual currencies, and I am sure professional currency traders can think of a lot more.

There must, of course, be a reason to speculate, something must occur for a dramatic shift in the perceptions of EMU or its individual currencies. Whatever you may tell people about apples equalling oranges, age old perceptions are extremely difficult to eradicate.

There are many fault lines inherent in EMU simply because of its composition. Originally it was planned that only 'responsible' countries enter, but by a long process of compromise, accident, and honest improvement, currencies, such as the lira, ended up being part of EMU. I believe that Italy should not have been included because there is too much potential for difficulty with it. However, the way the situation developed, no one could get around to telling the Italian government this. Entry into EMU became a matter of national pride rather than economic sensibility, and so it was admitted. The German Central Bank is known to be very worried about this, but they cannot say so in public. However, there caution has proved well-founded.

The Italian political system produces governments that are, to say the least, extremely fragile. The average government since World War II has lasted 49 weeks. In October 1998, the government fell by one vote. A new government was cobbled together within weeks, an odd mixture of reformed Marxists, socialists, and centrists. It is the 57th government since 1945, and, if things go well for it and it maintains the average, it will be gone within a year. Italy's budget is showing signs of expanding again after a crash diet necessary for EMU entry, which required sustainability in financial reform, but this has not happened in Italy's case. Already the new government has promised to refund the 'euro tax' that was levied in order to get the government's finances below the necessary 3 per cent deficit figure. It is farcical, the government raises money in taxation in 1997 to meet sustainable EMU criteria, and gives it back soon after. What is even more farcical, is that it said it was doing so, every other member of the EU knew what it was doing, and they still accepted the doctored figures Italy presented to gain entry into EMU. This is not a general criticism of Italy, which has a strong industrial base and great potential, and has made vast strides since the Mafia was, effectively, at the head of the government, but it cannot be compared with Germany.

In contrast to this, Chancellor Kohl stepped down in October 1998 after serving seventeen years, he was only the 7th German Chancellor since the end of World War II. Such differences in governmental stability may simply be too immense to merge into one currency. It will just take one, serious crisis in Italy for Italians to start changing currency. What if, instead of 100 professional speculators, you have a couple of million smaller ones. What if the Italian middle class want to move to the Deutschmark in order to protect their wealth. The Deutschmark has always been viewed as a safe currency. What if they physically start changing lira into Deutschmarks? It may very well be that both are sub-denominations of the euro, but what if they physically prefer to hold the German sub-denomination rather than the Italian sub-denomination? If the two currencies are supposedly equal, then they have a risk free bet. If the EMU proceeds, then the Deutschmark becomes the euro at the same relative rate as the lira, and they have lost nothing but minor transaction costs. If Italy somehow withdraws from EMU, then they will gain dramatically as the lira would plummet. Presenting rational people with a risk free option that can only be in their interest, will only encourage them to turn their lira into Deutschmarks at any provocation. If insurance is virtually free, then all rational people will take it. If you are worried about your home burning down, and a salesman knocks at your front door selling you fire insurance for next to nothing, then you would almost certainly take it.

If the lira started to be physically changed into Deutschmarks in increasing numbers, then the German government would become concerned. The reason for this concern is because it will be German banks who will be effectively required to send physical Deutschmarks to Italy in exchange for lira. The German government will be required to take more and more lira, and give more and more Deutschmarks for them. This is the real test of the euro, if the currencies are equal, then Germans should not care whether they have liras or Deutschmarks. While they would naturally initially play along with the game, at some point they would have to call a halt to it, unless they truly believe that the lira is the same as the Deutschmark, which every single German banker, in his heart of hearts, knows is not true.

In a free market of course, increased demand for Deutschmarks would lead to a rise in the number of lira needed to buy each Deutschmark, a rise in the value of the Deutschmark, and a fall in the value of the lira. But under EMU, the exchange rates are fixed. If the German government made any move to limit the flow of Deutschmarks, it would be an admission that the currencies are not equal. It would be a case of "all currencies are equal but some currencies are more equal than others". You can tell people that a Fiat is now equal to a Mercedes, and they may say they believe you, but when offered with a choice between the two, most will choose the Mercedes.

This is simply one currency link in many, that EMU requires to hold for three years for the system to survive. There are other currencies, such as the Portuguese escudo and Spanish peseta, that are, historically, weak currencies. EMU may very well function efficiently, and I hope it does, but it must prove itself for investors to believe in it. Until it does prove itself, many rational investors may simply decide to hold Deutschmarks when the natural incentive of higher interest rates for other currencies is gone. This is the main reason why there were higher interest rates in the first place, because, if you want someone to hold your weaker currency, you have to reward them for the risk they are taking.

What will happen in Ireland's case is difficult to say, our government would be cognisant of the immense implications of leaving EMU, and would fight to stay in. It is difficult to foresee any situation where we would be forced out of EMU, but it is not impossible to think it could happen. Overall I do not think scenario 2 will happen: even if Italy withdraws from EMU, Ireland will still hang in, but, once started, turmoil in EMU could be very hard to control. If Italy did leave, many other nationals, and speculators, might start physically converting weaker currencies into Deutschmarks. The argument from different nationals would be pretty simple, "Yes, I believe that all currencies are equal, so then it shouldn't matter which one I hold my small amount of wealth in." It is such that the rational actions of each individual creates the reality that the ECB will not admit to. European currencies are not equal until we have only one currency in circulation but the process of getting to a single currency might be impossible because of the inequality of the currencies. A strange paradox, but an understandable one.

For Ireland, there is one case where we might actually wish to leave EMU. This would occur if the punt, *vis-à-vis* the euro, fell against sterling, or if sterling fell against the punt. Whatever the talk about our trade with Europe, our trade with the UK is also vitally important. If sterling weakened to a situation of relative parity with the punt, or even weakened below parity, then this would have a serious impact on agricultural and some other industries. We could not devalue as we no longer have our own currency. I wonder how much pain the government could take?

Because of all the difficulty with harmonising currencies and the need to create a strong euro, I found it almost impossible to believe one fact that I discovered while doing research. I discovered that the euro notes, which will be issued in 2002, will not be the same. While much has been made of displaying the obverse side of all euro notes and coins, not much attention has been paid to the reverse side. This is because the reverse side will clearly indicate the notes national origin. When I was told this, I could not understand it. I could not believe after the monumental efforts that will be made to create a common currency, that each country could not go the whole way and create a truly single currency. Yet further research proved it true. There are going to be Italian euros, German euros and Dutch euros. Most proponents of the euro react extremely negatively to this classification, but if euros issued in Ireland have a harp on them, and euros issued in Germany have an eagle on them, then they will forever be identified with their national origin. Why was this done? I simply do not understand why a single currency could not have been made homogenous. I have my suspicions as to why this is, but I will not give vent to them. Suffice it to say, certain countries like the concept of fire escapes.

There is one other factor which merits discussion because it could amplify any world slowdown, as per scenario number 1, or even cause it. This is the millennium bug, also known as the Year 2000 problem, or Y2K problem. The Y2K problem, which has been given extensive coverage in the media, is the difficulty some computers are going to have dealing with the date 2000. It appears a minor, almost insignificant problem, but it is going to have some major impacts. No one is yet sure how large the impact is going to be. One of the world authorities on the problem is Peter de Jager, who believes it will have a serious impact on many firms who are not yet prepared to deal with it. Also, Cap Gemini[1] issued a very worrying report last year, which stated that many businesses and governments were sailing close to the wind with it.

Basically the Y2K problem stems from the fact that many computer programmes use two digits to describe the date in many areas. We all do it in the way we speak, the 60s the 70s, it is easy and natural to truncate the date. Why bother saying the 1960s, or 1970s it is a waste of time. For computers however, this is a problem, because in the year 2000 when performing simple calculations, it will calculate dates wrong. I was born in 1965 so hence, in the year 2000, a computer trying to find out my age has a programming line 'age = current year - year born' which should be 2000 minus 1965, correct answer 35. However the computer with only two digits will know only the last two digits. So my age will be 00 minus 65, or -65. Yes it is an incredibly small problem, but it has gargantuan implications for businesses that have millions of lines of computer code with many date and time calculations in them. It will affect telephone companies, airlines, banks, etc. These industries have been scrabbling to work out the problem but they are going to miss some of the errors, and some other firms are doing nothing because they do not think they have a problem. While computer programs can be changed, some programs are 'hard coded' in computer chips which are installed in lifts, telephones, oil rigs, etc. Suffice it to say, the Y2K problem is an unknown quantity that will impact the Irish economy, but the question is how much and how seriously? It could very well be the force that causes a world recession, rather than the Asian crisis.

---

1.   The Cap Gemini group is the largest European computer services and business consulting company.

13

Analysis and Adaptation for Consumers

The pessimist complains about the wind;
the optimist expects it to change;
the realist adjusts the sails.

William Arthur Ward

There may be a cyclical downturn facing the economy, but this does not necessarily mean that everyone is facing hard times, only those that have overextended themselves and are not prepared. *The Bible*, a book one can rarely quote when talking about economics, speaks of the seven years of plenty and seven years of famine. The survival during the seven years of famine, relied upon the prudent actions taken during the seven years of plenty. While Ireland's years of plenty may be coming to an end, there are still many actions that can be taken to ensure that the years of famine are not too harsh. Everyone is the master of his own fate, you do not have to follow the crowd over the cliff simply because you have followed them to the cliff's edge.

This chapter is essentially about the proactive measures which consumers can take in order to focus solely on their own finances. It is essential that each person gets a snapshot of their situation, not of anyone else's or the economy's. This is not an attempt to give specific investment or financial advice for consumers, I am not an accountant and not qualified to give such advice to Irish people. It is a broad analysis of finances, using acceptable criteria. It highlights those areas which history has demonstrated have become problem areas for many consumers.

The first step in any planning process is to ascertain exactly what the current situation is. In the case of the finances of a person or a family, this requires asking a few basic questions connected with income, expenditure, assets and liabilities. From these four simple questions we can derive quite an amount of information.

1.   How much money do you earn?

2.   How much money do you spend?

3.   How much money do you owe?

4.   What is the total value of your assets?

Each question quite often hides a menagerie of little facts and confusions.

HOW MUCH MONEY DO YOU EARN?

The answer to this should be a base salary figure, excluding bonuses, overtime and any other perks. If you cannot expect to receive a portion of your salary on an ongoing basis for any reason, then it is not income upon which you can rely. Overtime, no matter how much it is or how certain you think it is, cannot be considered on the same scale as basic income, which you will receive on a continuous basis. It is extra income that should be saved or spent as such, but not relied upon.

For people who earn a large part of their salary in commissions, or who are on contract work, it may be difficult to arrive at a precise reliable base figure for income, but some reasonably accurate, and conservative, average must be arrived at. The significant point is to arrive at a reasonably stable figure that can be expected as income for the coming year.

HOW MUCH MONEY DO YOU SPEND?

This figure is going to be composed of fixed and variable outgoings. Fixed expenses are composed of expenses such as rent, mortgage, car repayments to mention but a few. The foundation of the definition of 'fixed' are that they cannot be changed over the short-term, or are incurred automatically. All of the above expenses usually come into that category. You cannot change your mortgage in the short-term, you have to pay it. Cable television, for example, may seem trivial, but it represents one of those small expenses that is usually paid automatically from your bank account, and so is semi-fixed in that it does not take conscious effort to incur the cost. Weekly groceries would be a fixed expenditure, even though they vary. Pick an average amount and use this as a figure for it.

Variable expenses are those expenses that require conscious effort to incur, and could vary largely one week, or month, to the next. These could include socialising, clothes purchases, etc.

Your expenses could also be categorised separately into those that are necessary and basic to sustaining a certain standard of living, and those that might be considered surplus. It is a very good idea to list your expenses in order of importance. Most people obviously start with accommodation, food and such essentials and end up with the extravagant and comforting luxuries that make life worth living. The important point here is to have a list of expenses in the order of how important they are to you, and also an indication of whether they are fixed or variable.

It is not necessary to be precise to the penny or even the pound, just so that you have a roughly accurate idea of where all your money goes. It is also helpful if you have a separate list of direct debits and standing orders. There is sometimes confusion about the difference between the two. A standing order is an instruction to your bank to pay a fixed amount to another party at fixed intervals, usually monthly. A direct debit is the authority you have given to another party to take varying amounts of money out of your account to settle bills which vary each period, such as a telephone bill.

HOW MUCH MONEY DO YOU OWE?

This is a list of all your outstanding liabilities. This should be divided into short and long-term debt. If you have just received a telephone bill, then that is obviously a short-term debt as you must pay it within the next 30 days. If you owe £75,000 on your mortgage, that is long-term debt of not much relevance immediately and so it should be listed in long-term debt. Where is the line between short and long-term debt? This is a tough question which could be argued about for months. But to keep things simple, if you could be reasonably expected to pay the money in the next six months then call it short-term debt. To be prudent I would put overdrafts, credit card, store card debt into short-term debt. Term loans, car loans, I would put into long-term debt.

WHAT IS THE VALUE OF YOUR ASSETS?

Assets should be divided into liquid, and illiquid, roughly the equivalent of short and long-term debt. Physical cash is obviously the most liquid asset, followed by bank accounts, bonds and other such near-cash instruments.

Illiquid assets are assets which you may have difficulty turning into cash in a short period of time, your house, a painting your grandmother left you, your car, shares, etc. Shares could possibly be put in liquid assets, but extreme prudence obliges me to put them in with illiquid, as when you most require them, the market could be down.

The next question is, naturally, the valuation of these assets. Firstly, shares simply require that you get the newspaper out and find today's quotation. Secondly, estimate the value of your house and other assets, such as your car, etc., using comparisons. Finally, take 20 per cent off these figures. The reason for this is that most people overvalue their own assets, and ignore the costs of liquidating them into cash.

Just writing all of the above information down on one piece of paper, can be an extremely revealing exercise in itself. There is, however, more valuable insight which you can acquire with closer analysis.

1.   You can tell what your basic living expenses are easily, and you also tell what your basic income is. If, for whatever reason, the economy slowed down, could you live on your basic income without any extras? If you are part of a couple, could you cover your basic living expenses from one salary?

2.   Do your short-term debts exceed your liquid assets? If this is the case, then it is a significant indication that you could possibly be over-stretched. An excess of short-term debt over liquid assets, means that you could not pay off all your debts immediately, you are relying on some future income to do so. This all presupposes that you have future income, if you lost your job tomorrow then you could not pay off your short-term debt.

3.   If you do lose your job, you should have at least three months' living expenses set aside in liquid assets to tide you over. This means that, even if you conform with point

number 2, then you may still be on shaky ground. You should have liquid assets totalling all of your short-term debt plus three months' basic living expenses. In a perfect world, you should probably have six months' living expenses. Such a cushion could take a great amount of pressure off you. If you are looking for a new job, you should have breathing room so you can choose the best job, and not just take the first one that comes along.

4. You should also look at your overall debt position. Do your total assets exceed your total debt? If they do not, then you should be investigating urgently why this is so. If your short-term debt and liquid assets are in check, then the problem obviously lies with long-term debt and illiquid assets. Your house could be worth less than you paid for it, as could your car, or any other asset you borrowed money to buy.

5. Another facet of your income and expenditure of which you should be conscious, is the number of fixed outgoings that are not essential. If you need to reduce your spending on non-essentials, will you be able to do so? It is easy to build up small commitments that are taken automatically from your bank account. They may be payments for cable television, a fitness club, a mobile phone, etc. You may find when you go to cut these, that they are contractual obligations for a set period, or that you must give a number of months' notice to cancel them. Businesses do this so that they themselves are not faced with a sudden contraction of income. You should, however, be aware that your ability to 'pull in your horns' may be not be what you think it is. Overextending yourself financially, does not just mean spending too much, it also means incurring fixed commitments which can become a financial liability if your income suddenly shrinks.

6. You should calculate how much of your expenditure is loan repayments and how much of this is exposed to interest rate fluctuations and other loan parameters. How much of it can be called in immediately? An overdraft can be called in at a moment's notice, whereas a term loan might not be. If banks want to limit exposure, the first thing they may do is start calling in overdrafts. On the other hand, you should also look at what debt you can pay off immediately if you so wish. People quite often think that if you

are willing to pay off a loan, then the creditor will be only too eager to take the money. Think again. As far as they are concerned, the money is 'deposited' with you, and you may be paying a very high interest rate to them, so why should they want it back in this low interest rate environment. You always have to look at these things from both sides.

By now you should have a fair reckoning on your financial situation. There are very few fixed rules, but by writing down all your finances on one sheet of paper and examining a few points, most people can gauge if they are overstretched or not.

The next part of this chapter is broken into two sections. The first part is composed of some simple financial pointers which we all should be able to benefit from. They should give you flexibility and allow you to react to any economic downturn as you see fit.

Part two is a set of strategies for reducing expenditure in the face of an economic downturn. They provide a framework upon which you can build and expand to suit your own needs. It is important to remember that it is not what you earn, but what you spend. The person who earns £40,000 and spends £41,000 is in a worse position than the person who earns £10,000 and spends £8,000.

GENERAL FINANCIAL SUGGESTIONS

Interest Rates

Be conscious of interest rates when borrowing and saving. In today's interest rate environment, it is quite possible that you are only receiving between 1 and 2 per cent for money you have on deposit. If you have outstanding debt at higher rates, such as credit card debt, then you are probably wiser to pay it off. Some credit cards charge up to 20 per cent on outstanding balances, and I have even seen some store cards currently charging up to 30 per cent. Paying this level of interest is crazy, especially if you have cash on deposit. Pay off all the debt you can while obviously leaving yourself with enough cash. Paying off debt is the same as putting the money on deposit, only you get a better rate.

If you must borrow money, then do so from a bank or building society. A term loan from a bank will be cheaper than from most other sources. It is easy to be talked into looking only at repayments; ask to see all the details. What is the rate? How much interest are you going to be paying? What will your total repayments be? Consider fixing the interest rate on whatever loans you have, as fixed interest rates give you predictability and certainty.

Save and Invest

Even if the interest rates are low, saving is a good habit to develop, be it in a post office account or, over the long-term, in the stock market. In times of plenty and prosperity, saving becomes out of vogue, it is fashionable to consume in the expectation that the time of plenty will continue. Fortune is always on the side of the prudent.

Own your Own Home

Even though house prices have rocketed up, they will fall again to reasonable levels. A home of your own is always a solid investment for the long-term. However while prices are at the current levels, I would bide my time, although each person must follow their own opinions.

Invest in Education

The more you know, the more specialised you are and the more you can demand for your skills. Do not stop learning when you leave school or university. Take every course and avail of every opportunity to develop yourself and hone your skills. It will pay handsome financial rewards.

STRATEGIES FOR RETRENCHMENT

Cutting expenditure is much easier than people believe it to be, what is difficult is living with the cuts. Most financial problems are caused by the perpetuation of spending patterns that are not suitable to a person's income. It is best that spending is cut quickly, procrastination just makes the problem worse. However, spending tends to be 'sticky' – once it goes up, it is hard to rein it in. The most difficult aspect of cutting expenditure is usually pride and "keeping up with the Jones"; once these are overcome, it is plain sailing. There are ten simple ways to cut spending.

1. **Work out what are essentials and what are non-essentials.** It is amazing how much clutter we have in our lives which we do not need and are probably better off without. Once you have discovered what are essentials, then set a budget and stick with it. If you have a partner, then both of you must be involved in setting the budget, it is not good enough for one of you to be economising while the other is splurging.

2. **If you have short-term debt, then start paying it off and pay off as much as you can, as fast as you can.** The quicker you reduce your debt, the less of your income is wasted on interest payments, late fees and penalty payments.

3. **If you feel your debt is too burdensome, then go straight to your creditors and discuss the situation.** Most creditors will bend over backwards to help a borrower who is honest and straightforward with them. You will be amazed to find out how reasonable most creditors can be. Avoiding creditors does nothing but create more problems.

4. **Consolidate all of your debt into one loan, if such an option is available to you.** The interest rate for such loans, especially those secured on your property, is much lower than other debt. If possible, dispose of all your store and credit cards and limit yourself to one.

5. **Jettison the unnecessary payments that are draining your bank account.** Ask your bank for a list of all standing orders and direct debits. Stop all but the essentials. Big ships are sunk by small leaks.

6. **Pay for everything that you can in cash. Paying in cash makes you think about it, cheques and credit cards are too painless.** If you are in financial difficulty, you need to deal in cash. Using a fixed amount of cash is also an easy way of keeping to a budget.

7. **Examine your three highest expenditures to see if you could possibly save money.** These are usually mortgage/rent, weekly groceries and transport. Talk to your financial institution about ways to reduce your mortgage. Any reduction in your mortgage is naturally just shifting debt around in different time periods, but in the short-term, if you need breathing room it can be a good idea. Buy all of your groceries in the supermarket, and buy generic products – many generic products are branded products in different wrappers.

8. **If you have a car, consider getting rid of it. Consider it carefully, but consider it.** In cities such as Dublin, cars are becoming a costly accessory that is not necessary. A good bike and your legs are not only much cheaper, but healthier. A reduction in monthly expenditure, possibly a capital inflow from the sale of the car, and a healthier body, is a definite win-win-win situation.

9. **If you have to live somewhat frugally for a year or two, then make it a productive time, enjoy it.** Take some night-classes, they are usually cheap and keep you entertained. Learn to cook, and eat at home instead of eating out. Cooking your own food is not only enjoyable, but incredibly inexpensive. If you want to then take up beer brewing or wine making, it is reasonably cheap, fun to do and the final product can save you money as well. You do not have to live like a monk, you can easily shave 25 per cent or more off your monthly expenditure and have more fun than ever.

10. **Do not be penny wise and pound foolish.** Think hard and long before you cut expenses such as health or life insurance. Do not lose sight of the fact that you are trying to reshape your expenditure, do not just cut for the sake of cutting.

14

Analysis and Adaptation for Business

The successful man is the one who
finds out what is the matter with his
business before his competitors do.

Roy L Smith

A business owner is in somewhat more of a dilemma than a private individual. A consumer could totally ignore any reckless abandonment that is taking place around him, and live life in pretty much the same way as before. For a business owner or manager, this is not necessarily an option. When the activity in a economy starts increasing, then it is normal that most businesses feel the surge and quite often they must expand with it.

An increase in turnover may appear to be just what any business wants. Who can resist an opportunity to make more money, isn't this what most people are in business for? Well the answer to that is yes and no, the desire of any business is to make sustainable profits, not just profits. A business, which chases profits in the short-term, at the cost of long-term profits, is not acting rationally. The function of this chapter is to illustrate the factors people should be aware of during expansion, and more importantly, the warning signs that occur when a business may be overextended. It also discusses the methods which a business can use to retrench in the face of an economic downturn. The ability to retrench quickly is a sign of good management planning.

The key to a business' survival is how well it expands in the face of growth, and how quickly it contracts in the face of a downturn in business. A business person must be able to expand quickly to capture the largest share of the market and then contract equally quickly when a downturn comes. A business that expands to meet a certain level of demand, which then dissolves away, can be left in dire circumstances if there are fixed costs. For example, a well known chain store in the UK expanded during the boom in the late-1980s, but it did this by signing contracts for new shops without allowing an inexpensive way to get out of those contracts. When demand dropped away rapidly, and they needed to close unprofitable stores, they could not. These unprofitable stores were pulling down the overall profitability, and viability, of the chain.

The problems that businesses encounter in dealing with expansion/contraction are as follows.

1. The business owner may believe that the expansion in business is permanent, and cannot see any possibility for a change in circumstances. This is a bad mistake to make, not simply because business is cyclical, but because a manager should have sufficient theoretical training and experience to understand market dynamics.

2. A business may be in an industry where expansion is rigid and not flexible. The example quoted previously in this book about the restaurant and the brewery, is a example of this. The rigidity of expansion is a eternal dilemma for business. How can I expand efficiently while still being able to contract, is a question managers often ask themselves. The answer, in many cases, may be that you cannot – expansion must be undertaken or not undertaken, certain industries offer this stark choice. The craft of management should be to try to make expansion as flexible as possible even in industries where expansion is normally extremely rigid.

3. Quite often a business may feel that it has to expand, because of competition. New entrants, or other market members, may be planning to expand if you are not. This perception that you have to expand, should be examined closely. Quite often, letting your competition develop before you can be an extremely competitive move, as you can learn from their mistakes.

4. Firms, which wish to expand, might not have the ability to do so, or it may be prohibitively expensive. In the up-cycle of a boom, the price of assets and labour tends to rise. Depending on your specific business, you may need certain resources for which you are forced into competing. The price of these may rise to such a level that the extra benefit they produce to your business is negated by their cost.

5. A cyclical rise in business may be the impetus you need for a long-awaited expansion. If you can expand and reduce

your average cost per unit, then you might use the demand in the boom as a cushion while you attempt to break into other markets. An exporter for example, could expand and use the extra cyclical demand as a cushion while he hammers away at certain export markets with his lower cost units. Hopefully by the time domestic demand falls away, he has established himself in other markets that are somewhat contra-cyclical to the domestic ones.

The above discussion is composed of broad theoretical points, and is merely food for thought for many business people. What is much more relevant and important, is the ability of a manager to spot signs of overexpansion so that they can take action. Even in the full summer of a boom, a manager should always be cognisant that the seasons will change and they should be alert to signs of overexpansion and/or inefficiency. Trimming and control at this early stage always makes contraction, and adjustment at a later stage much easier. Signs of overexpansion include:

- lack of control;

- human resource problems;

- inventory problems;

- cash flow disguising problems with profitability.

During booming business times, it is easy to let management of the small things slip away. In many cases, staff may increase but not management, or, even if management does increase, the owner or general manager is still only one person. An essential function of management is control, and controlling growth is an extremely skilful operation. In boom times, costs can creep up, and profitability can diminish, but this is difficult to detect because, overall, the absolute profit figure will be rising. Turnover can hide a lot of problems that would otherwise be exposed.

The solution to this is to have a good management/accounting system in place that can accurately keep track of the most significant costing details. It is a critical component of any business that precise information be sought out. Business may well feel like it is booming but that may not be the case. A pilot recently told me that 90 per cent of the time an airliner is going in the wrong direction; if you were to draw a straight line in the direction the plane is pointed, then it would not arrive where it is meant to be. The plane is buffeted by many factors that cannot be known in advance, however, the on-board computers adjust every couple of minutes to keep the plane on course. If the computers did not do this frequently, the plane would go seriously off track. Most businesses are the same, most of the time they are pointed in the wrong direction and need constant attention to keep them on track. The target being sustainable profitability.

When business increases, it is normal that staff numbers also increase, what is important is to ensure that staff turnover costs do not escalate unduly. If business is growing fast, it is only natural to hire staff but the quality of hiring decisions should not suffer. Pressures are sometimes high to find someone – anyone – and quite often there is not much choice, especially when skills are in such short supply that prospective staff can have the upper hand. However, the costs of an increase in the staff turnover can be greater than not having anyone.

If new staff members need to be trained, there will be a certain period in which they will not have reached full productivity. These costs are acceptable as long as the employees are going to stay, but if you are turning over staff quickly, these expenses can become extremely burdensome.

Quite often it is extremely difficult to avoid higher staff turnover in a boom, simply because employees start to play musical chairs. The more people begin to think that their job is secure, the more they are willing to change jobs. It is one of those strange paradoxes of employment, that in uncertain economic times everyone wants job security, and in boom times when they have it, then they want to change jobs. It is reasonable that people move jobs, and seek to develop themselves and their careers, however, quite often the movement is caused by a desire for short-term higher remuneration. This, again, is a reasonable desire, but it can incur unnecessary costs for employers competing with each other. Managers should watch closely the costs associated with hiring and training staff.

One other relevant aspect of human resources is 'temping' agencies. In a boom these organisations tend to proliferate like rabbits. While these businesses play an important role in the economy, they are only good in moderation. Quite often in a boom, the temping agencies are contracting out employees who would otherwise be working in a full-time job. If all temping workers picked one firm, then there would not be a need for temporary workers. Yes, this simplifies things immensely, but the point is that temping agencies sometimes create the void which they profess to fill. They make a handsome cut, the employee makes more money in the short-term, but the costs are endured by business, and added to the final product. Inflationary and non-productive middlemen is an extremely harsh description of temping agencies, but in boom times this is sometimes what they are.

Vast numbers of articles have been written on inventory levels during the various phases of the business cycle, and it is neither my function or intent to go into a complex analysis of inventory levels on an industry by industry basis. The important concerns with inventory levels can be highlighted with two basic points.

1.   Inventory build up creates many problems.

2.   Inventory is not cash, but it may be reflected so in accounts.

At the start of an upturn in the economy, inventory levels begin to diminish, sometimes until there is rationing. In many cases, customers increase orders from suppliers, and suppliers then increase orders from manufacturers to balance this. This growing optimism eventually rises to vastly over-optimistic ordering, and subsequent demands from manufacturing. This has a positive impact for manufacturers, until one day someone realises that the inventory has grown too much for current demand. Orders are then cut, or skipped, throughout the chain which brings a general slowdown.

The important point is to keep control on inventories. Managers should design forecasting systems that can better predict demand. I realise that this is an easy thing to say, and it is near impossible to get right, but be aware of letting inventory build up. Every time you are ordering, ask yourself are you overdoing it, apply rigid criteria to orders and involve more people in the decision to try to achieve a balance, be wary of automatic ordering systems, which have not been fine tuned.

Inventory is not cash, although accountants quite often may deem it so. Inventory was paid for in cash, or is owed for in cash, but it is a businesses job to turn inventory into cash. Inventory hides many products that may be difficult to liquefy to cash. In a boom, this problem may grow, as more products creep into the system that may be difficult to sell. One computer distributor in the US had millions in dollars in stock on his books, yet when auditors went in after the firm went into liquidation, they found that computers were overvalued. What was top of the line twelve months ago, was nearly redundant now. It should be a warning sign if you have inventory that is depreciating quickly. Even if it is not depreciating, the larger the level of inventory you carry, the larger the carrying costs are.

The bottom line is that no matter how well a large section of inventory is turning over, if you have 'silt' building up in inventory it is a potential sign of trouble for when the economy slows. Watch both your stock, and your stock levels, control the inflow of 'silt', and realistically value the stock you have.

Cash flow is probably a greater cause of difficulty for many firms than inventory. Cash flow is an extremely visible number, it is easy to calculate for most businesses, but it indicates nothing about the profitability of the firm. In a boom, cash flow may rise quickly, but so too do many costs. It again requires strong management accounting practices to ascertain if profitability is being maintained, or hopefully increased. Profit is the key indicator for a business, not cash flow.

The next section of this chapter is probably the most important, because it contains suggestions on how to control the problems that affect businesses once a downturn starts. The problems of course, can probably be summed up in one word: money. If turnover starts to fall, then you need to start reorganising fast to control expenses. During a boom, expansion usually occurs, and inefficiencies set in; during a downturn, you either make changes or go out of business.

The Americans are masters of cutting costs which is why many American firms have survived through many business cycles. They will expand very quickly during the up-cycle, but once the downturn occurs, they will cut costs ruthlessly. American management does not confuse itself about what they are trying to do, they are trying to survive. There are turnaround specialists who, in dire times, come into firms to cut costs and save the firms from bankruptcy. Employees tend to call them hatchetmen, but they are doing a vital job.

There are seven basic rules to cutting costs in a downturn. Everything naturally depends on the type of business, the size of the business and the seriousness of your problems. These are broad rules, not specific advice. It is a manager's job, in conjunction with the appropriate financial experts, to solve specific problems. However, these basic rules will illuminate areas of interest for most managers.

1.   Find the fat fast, and cut it.

2.   Cut staff.

3.   Renegotiate any leases you have.

4.   Negotiate with the tax authorities.

5.   Find capital goods that consume expenditure.

6.   Cut product lines.

7.   Spend on the important things.

The 'fat' is what has grown up over the good times, the excesses that have crept in and which must now be cut. The faster they are cut, the better. Take a look at every cheque, direct debit, and other outgoing from the last three months, and I guarantee that you will find that at least 10 per cent are wasteful. Question every outgoing, find out what is was spent on and why. Ask yourself, does this contribute directly to the bottom line? Every industry and business will be different, but common areas of fat include the following.

- **Travel expenses.** Car rental, airlines, hotels can quite often milk business travellers. Examine your travel expenses closely, using on-line services, such as www.travelocity.com for booking travel which can save quite an amount of money. Never travel business class, unless there are specific reasons. It is a waste of money, for very little extra.

- **Advertising, promotion and sponsorship**. Someone once said that 50 per cent of advertising money was wasted, the problem is that no one knows which 50 per cent. However, I suggest that you try to find out which 50 per cent. Promotion and sponsorship are very grey areas, with which I am never really comfortable. If you cannot see an identifiable return, then cut it and see if business is affected. If it is, then resume it, if it isn't then you just saved some money.

- **Entertainment expenses.** Who is being entertained and why? Freeloaders expand with turnover.

Generally speaking, when someone is spending your money there is a dilemma. It isn't their money, and even if they save money, it does not make any difference to them. I have seen some crazy expense systems that actually ended up penalising people for saving money for their company. You have to make your staff think about saving your money, and the best way is usually via monetary reward. Design a system that rewards people for saving money. You could, for example, reward them with a third of the total savings they make.

Also implement a reward system for identifying waste, and abuse. Money is a great motivator. Once people get a cut, you will really begin to notice a difference. It is fairly crude, but effective.

If business is falling off, then staff need to be shed. Staff may be your largest expense, so it has to be dealt with rapidly and there should be no procrastination about it. It is tough job, but effective management requires tough decisions. Is it better that you cut 20 per cent of your staff, or keep them on and let the firm go bankrupt with the loss of 100 per cent? The 20 per cent are not going to be happy, but the 80 per cent will understand. Labour laws in Ireland are not as oppressive as Europe, so staff can be shed relatively inexpensively. Explain to the 20 per cent why you are doing it, and also explain to the 80 per cent what you are doing. It is important to make the remaining staff feel secure.

Picking which staff to shed is naturally a purely case by case decision, however there should be some method to it. Using policies such as 'last in – first out' is really a random system. Keep the best and most productive, do not jettison them just because you wish to follow an arbitrary system that alleviates guilt.

If you are leasing property, equipment or motor vehicles then do not accept these costs as set in concrete. Approach the landlord or whoever and seek to renegotiate. A landlord will be acutely aware of the economic conditions and will not wish to risk losing a sitting tenant or customer for the sake of 10-20 per cent of a lease. While your contract may oblige you in law to pay certain amounts, a landlord will also realise that if you go bankrupt because of his lease, he is just going to be another unsecured creditor.

Negotiate with the Revenue Commissioners – they are always the last to be paid when times turn sour, simply because they actually provide 'nothing' for the payment. Businesses quite often used money earmarked for the Revenue as working capital, but this is a dangerous game to play because they can get very nasty, very quickly and the sheriff can be on your doorstep before you know it. Yet they also can be extremely flexible, if you talk to them before things get out of hand. They can provide you with short-term finance if you are on good terms with them.

Many businesses have capital goods that are consuming heavy resources on an annual basis with such things as service contracts, extended guarantees, professional staff on retainers, and a cacophony of strange fees for which little is produced. The usual culprits can be photocopiers, computers, and other specialised equipment. Management may have very little knowledge about these pieces of equipment, and have been worried into signing service contracts simply because they fear huge bills. Do research, learn about this equipment, find out how often they fail. Find out if you really need as sophisticated a machine as you think you do. I know of one company that disposed of five photocopiers worth close to a quarter of a million dollars, and kept one small model – and they never noticed the difference. They simply went into a local print shop whenever they needed a large jobs done and negotiated good rates with them. It is amazing how much photocopying really costs, and how much work disappears when someone has to request a job specifically. The key point is to question all expenses, which appear to be basic necessities as, quite often, they are not.

Computers are another big culprit. While I am a great believer in the cost savings that many computers can bring, I have also seen many cases where computers are voracious consumers of resources. Quite often, businesses are fleeced by computer companies who overload them with too many computers that are too sophisticated for their needs. Software is another area where computer companies make a lot of revenue. Upgrading to the next version is quite often not necessary, I am quite sure that 75 per cent of the features on most software programs are never used in the first place, so why upgrade? I have a good rule of thumb for computers: if it is working and doing what you want, then leave the system alone. Forget new machines and new software unless your staff are specifically asking for them, and justifying it. Examine all service contracts for computers. Most modern electronics never fail; if they do, they can be fixed. You don't have a service contract for cars or televisions, so unless there are specific reasons, don't have them for computers. If it breaks, call out a service person and get it fixed. Many computer companies use fear and lack of knowledge to sell service contracts and other unnecessary products.

Consumers' taste tend to expand with a boom, and contract with the down-cycle. A firm that has been catering to consumers tastes might find substantial savings in reducing product lines. A close examination is required to see which product lines earn money, and which ones do not. If, for example, you are selling a range of 50 ties, you may discover that twenty of them do 70 per cent of the business and the other 30 absorb production time, confuse salespeople and distributors, and generally absorb effort for little return. Furthermore, you may find that sales might only drop slightly as customers simply redistribute orders over the smaller product range. The decision to cut a product range will, of course, require much consultation and investigation. A wide product range may be essential to maintaining sales.

Cutting expenses in a downturn is vital, but you should not get too far ahead of the curve. Some expenses are valid and necessary, even if they may seem frivolous. Sometimes money simply has to be spent, in ways that appear wasteful, in order to obtain orders. The skill of a cost cutter is to be able to differentiate the muscle from the fat.

15

Silver Lining

I buy when everyone is selling.

J P Getty

The secret of many a billionaire, is moving in and mopping up after the excesses of the crowd. Many fortunes have been made by people who had the tenacity and self-confidence to buy when nobody else is buying. We are strange creatures in that we always want what it was difficult to acquire, but rarely want what is easy to acquire, even when it is what we wanted when it was difficult to get. There is nothing like a crowd of people to stimulate buying. Every single one of us are drawn to a crowd, just to see what they are looking at. We surmise that if everyone else wants it, then it must be good.

People, such as Getty, Hearst, Rockefeller and many others like them, have known that the secret to wealth is to buy when nobody else is buying. It sounds easy, but it isn't. When everybody is telling you that something is a bad idea, then most people listen. The men above did not listen, and that is what made them wealthy. When Ireland's boom expires, there are going to be tremendous bargains to be had by those with the resources and foresight to buy. Acquiring the foresight simply requires astuteness and self-confidence; the resources, however, are another matter.

Banks that are throwing money at you in the boom, will suddenly not want to give it to you. A friend of mine in the UK told me how during the housing boom his building society would have loaned him £200,000 to buy an apartment in London, but during the slump, they would not give him £150,000 to buy a house there. This, of course, is part of the reason why houses were cheap – without the financial institutions pouring money into the housing market, many people could not buy. It is highly ironic, but that is the way it has been around the world and that is the way it will be in Ireland. The word 'caution' will enter the vocabulary of lenders and only the strongest candidates will get any kind of credit. This leaves the bargain hunting to those with their own resources, or with enough credibility to extract credit from the reluctant financial institutions. Money makes money.

Once the down-cycle hits and begins to accelerate, there will be many bargains to be had. I will look briefly now at the three main types.

- Houses.

- Commercial property.

- Medium-priced assets.

Houses in Ireland have been a classic asset bubble and the collapse will probably be as spectacular as the rise. In most cases where real estate rocketed up, then the fall was always equally overdone. I expect a fall of around 40 per cent in house prices in Dublin, and in some cases possibly even more. It will all depend on being in the right place at the right time.

The question in all downturns is knowing when the bottom has been reached, and what indicators one should look out for. Defining the bottom of a cycle, is like defining the top of one. The only indicator I watch for is the point of 'maximum pessimism' when all the scribes and 'experts' are telling you that the prices are going to keep falling forever and that the economy is bad and getting worse. The papers will be full of horror stories about negative equity, about how investments in property went bad and the such like. In the case of residential property, there will be extremely visible signs like wide-scale repossessions, headline evictions, and a backlash against the financial institutions that lent the money in the first place. In the case of Ireland, there will also probably be a government committee of some kind set up.

Wherever the bottom is precisely, there are going to be ample bargains in the housing market for those with the resources to exploit them. In the heat of the boom, you currently have to queue up to hand your deposit cheque to a auctioneer or developer (and you are probably going to end up being gazumped anyway). However, once the down-cycle has gathered pace, the buyer with cash will be king. I predict that the person who walks into most auctioneers in Dublin with £150,000 in liquid funds, will have the majority of the property on the auctioneer's books within their grasp. Liquid funds, i.e. cash, will multiply your leverage two or three-fold simply because many sellers will be desperate to sell.

The process of selling a house in Dublin will slow down immeasurably, because many buyers will be tangled up in getting approval sorted out from the now overcautious lenders, or be tied to what is known as 'a chain'. A chain is where you are selling your house and moving up, but have to wait for your sale to close in order for you in turn to close your purchase. Quite often the person you are selling your house to is in a similar bind. An interesting documentary on the BBC in the early 1990s traced back one chain through seven different sets of sellers and buyers. The end of the chain was someone questionable who had not yet been approved for his mortgage, he was finally refused so withdrew his offer, and this cascaded up the line and 'collapsed' all the deals.

Those with cash can leapfrog all of this to capitalise on eager sellers. If an auctioneer knows you have cash, he will be more eager to deal with you because he knows a sale can be closed within days, and his commission is assured.

The difficult aspect of this, is that you may be dealing with people who are desperate to sell because they got in over their heads during the boom. While gazumping is all the talk on the way up, gazundering will be the seller's prerogative on the way down. Pressurising desperate people to cut the price may not be everyone's cup of tea, but all I can say is that the market must be kept efficient if it is to function. If you feel you can get something for less than the asking price, then so be it.

Building societies and banks may also be stuck with foreclosed properties, as they were in the UK, and they will not wish to hold them. Financial institutions are just that, they deal in money, and they do not wish to become landlords. Watch for sales from these places, as they will be in the market to unload property, before they become bogged down in maintaining unoccupied houses and dealing with squatters. They are not going to hold on for the upturn, it is not their role.

Many people cannot, of course, accept that the housing market will turn around so quickly, from a state where people are clamouring to buy, to a bargainhunters' paradise. The fact is that the demand will diminish, and supply increase for a number of basic reasons.

1.   Those who bought high, cannot re-enter the market as they have no funds so they are out of the equation.

2.   Expatriates will not be flowing into an economy that has slowed, and they may be flowing out again. Less demand.

3.   If a mortgage cannot be paid due to unemployment, property will be foreclosed and end up on the market very quickly.

4.   Negative media stories will deter many people from buying out of fear that their jobs are not secure.

5.   Financial institutions will have been burnt, and will be shy about lending, further reducing demand.

6.   Speculators in the property market will be unloading further supply as they too experience financial difficulty, and desire to get out of a falling market.

7.   The bottlenecks with supply will probably be breached and deliver large quantities of houses on to the market at exactly the wrong time (not for buyers, of course).

Commercial property will also suffer a similar downturn, but not everyone will wish to exploit this. Only those interested in a specific area of business will be willing to move in. Again the problem will be funding, unless you have cash, or can extract a loan from someone, you will not be able to exploit the situation.

One example of commercial property, which I feel could be exposed to the full wrath of a downturn, will be the hotel industry. As demonstrated earlier in the book, hotels are probably going to suffer from the cobweb syndrome. This is where supply, which was initiated in the boom, overtakes waning demand. Already with the economy showing signs of slowing down, there are still hotels that have not come into operation. If demand has slackened, you will see some hotels forced into liquidation and this will be time for any astute operator to move in. If you can buy heavily discounted hotel property, and wait for the up tick, then handsome profits are to be made.

Many medium-priced consumer goods that were bought during the boom will probably flood the market. This category includes cars, boats, expensive electronics and other home appliances. This occurs in down-cycles for three reasons.

1. They were bought on credit and the purchaser cannot keep up the repayments.

2. They were bought with cash, but now the owner needs cash for more urgent reasons.

3. Supplier who overstocked in the boom will be discounting to sell stock.

Many people overextend themselves during a boom, and borrow money which they cannot afford. If they lose their jobs, or simply cannot keep up repayments, then they will try to sell these assets, especially if they are assets that further consume resources. If a car was just a capital expenditure, then most people could have two or three. However, a car needs road tax, petrol, parking and insurance. This can make holding a car a liability in a time of financial hardship.

An increase in the supply of certain assets will do two things – drive the price down and, equally, affect whatever sales are still existing for the retailers. This will, in turn, force some retailers out of business. During the boom, the retailer was not only supplying increased demand from natural growth, but effectively supplying future demand by selling to people who could not afford the asset in the long-term, or even, probably, who could not afford it in the short-term. People often confuse being able to afford something, with having the money to buy it.

If the retailer assumed that this level of demand could be maintained, then he may have expanded to meet it. Expansions based on maintaining the high sales levels experienced in a boom, are difficult. This is why those stable firms that resist expansion and do not incur debt, may outlive those that build flashy new premises on borrowed money. The net result of this will probably be a bumper business for the classified adds and such magazines as *Buy & Sell*.

Conclusion

The conclusion to this book is being written in the opening days of 1999. I spent time in Ireland over the last couple of weeks, and I was not encouraged by what I saw. The level of intoxication in the economy has reached near epidemic proportions and no one is showing any signs of caution. I spent some time talking to various friends and acquaintances to gauge the mood, and not much has changed. The optimistic news is gushing forth in the media and people are spending like there is no tomorrow.

Three interesting points struck me as highly significant and I will discuss them here. They also serve nicely as a conclusion, as they are a microcosm of much of what this book has been about.

The first of these was the availability of quick and 'emergency' credit. A small 'financial shop' on one of the main streets of Dublin was offering immediate credit of £500 on the production of a cheque book. An advance on a person's salary to the end of the month was also available on the production of a salary slip. This kind of credit marked the outer limits of the boom in London, and it is the first time I have seen it offered so prominently in Dublin, and it would not be there unless there was demand for it. It is credit for middle class people who are obviously stretched to the limit everywhere else and are caught in a spiral and robbing Peter to pay Paul. The cost of such credit would be, I presume, close to the maximum legal limit. This point, and other such indicators, I noticed reinforced my opinion that a significant number of people are living close to the edge of the cliff with credit. I spoke to people who are not earning particularly large salaries and they spoke of the pressure to spend to keep up with their friends (the cost of socialising in Dublin is frightening), many were borrowing in varying guises in order to do this. This simply cannot last. There is true economic growth in Ireland, but there is also much pseudo-prosperity.

The second point I noticed was just how bad the traffic in Dublin is. I find it amazing that anyone can conduct business in such an environment. On a cold, rainy morning I hopped on a bus going towards the city centre, but the traffic jam was such that the bus only served as a temporary respite from the rain. Three others like myself got on, they shook down their coats, dried out as best they could, and then made a few phone calls explaining their absence from wherever they should have been. After strumming their fingers for a while, they got off the bus and proceeded on foot – their walking exceeding the speed of the bus. I, eventually, joined them in the rain, I simply could not afford to waste anymore time on public transport. I also spent inordinate amounts of time in Dublin trying to hail down taxis. In the end, the inability to transport myself around the city forced me to rent a car for the last few days of my stay, I could rely on neither public nor private transport so I was forced, like so many others, to contribute to the problem.

The third, and most important point, is that apartment prices in Dublin fell for the first time in years. Much effort was made in the media to explain this away as some normal adjustment, or some seasonal correction, however it is what it is, the start of the decline in property prices. Apartment prices have peaked, and are now probably on the way down, houses will follow in due course. There must now already be people in Dublin who paid more for their apartment than it is worth – negative equity may have appeared on the horizon.

The above three points highlight the dilemma that many Irish people find with their new found chaotic prosperity.

I have considered carefully the idea that the Irish economy is in some 'new mode', or that a historic shift has occurred, and I am not convinced. I rely on hundreds of years of economic theory and many analogies before anything else. Because of EMU-induced interest rate cuts, a strong economy received the equivalent of steroid injections, and has become wildly distorted. The excessive and unnatural growth has been accompanied by excessive optimism and irrational exuberance, which has further exacerbated the problem. Prompted by lower interest rates, many consumers have gone on a spending binge. The myth of the Celtic Tiger has, in their minds, guaranteed their jobs so they feel they can extend themselves financially. These actions, in the short-term, extend the boom, but they also put inordinate amounts of pressure on physical infrastructure that simply cannot expand with consumers' spending power.

Sharp, rapid expansions such as we are witnessing in Ireland are nearly always followed by sharp contractions when reality, in all its forms, catches up with consumers. I see no reason why matters will be any different in Ireland. In the short-term, the boom will continue, but in the medium-term, a fairly severe contraction must occur.

So as not to conclude on such a pessimistic note, I am optimistic about the long-term future of the Irish economy. Once we can recover from any medium-term recession, and differentiate ourselves from Europe sufficiently to maintain and attract foreign investment, we have a bright future.

Bibliography

Preparing for Economic and Monetary Union: A Guide for Business Ulster Bank 1997.

Harper W Boyd & Orville C Walker, *Marketing Management: A Strategic Approach* (Richard D Irwin) 1990.

Professor Robert Dailey *et al*, *Organisational Behaviour* (London: Pitman Publishing) 1995.

Hugh Fleming & Andrew Scott, *International Trade and Finance* (London: Pitman Publishing) 1995.

John Kenneth Galbraith, *The Affluent Society* (Boston: Mariner Books) 1958.

Peter de Jager & Richard Bergeon, *Managing 00: Surviving the Year 2000 Computing Crisis* (New York: John Wiley & Sons) 1997.

Charles P Kindleberger, *Manias, Panics and Crashes* (New York: John Wiley & Sons) 1978.

Mark Kishlansky, Geary Patrick & Patricia O'Brien, *Civilisation in the West* (New York: Harper Collins) 1991.

Steven E Landsburg, *The Armchair Economist* (New York: The Free Press) 1993.

Lars Tvede, *Business Cycles: From John Law to Chaos Theory* (Amsterdam: Hardwood Academic Publishers) 1997.

The Caring Economy:
Internet Business Principles

Gerry McGovern

The Caring Economy is based on a number of fundamental beliefs. These beliefs are that the forthcoming digital age demands new thinking and a new philosophy, requires a new set of business principles, governing everything from research and development to customer interaction, and is a time when technology will become transparent and people will become paramount.

If businesses want long-term success in the digital age, they need to care about people, and about the issues that are important to people. The Internet is a revolution in communications, and not in technology. This is not a book about computers or the Internet, nor is it about bandwidth, faster processors, information technology, e-commerce, digital television, video on demand, nerds and hackers. It is not about cost savings and downsizing and automating people out of the picture. *The Caring Economy* covers and explores all these technologies and issues, but it is not about them.

It is rather a book about people - both business people and consumers - and how we all interact with each other, in life and on the Internet. It explores the relationship between people and the tools they make and use. It seeks to establish some philosophical foundations and basic principles for living in the digital age.

The book is written from the standpoint that community and commerce are inherently intertwined - you cannot have one without the other. It explores the whole meaning of what a 'network' is, what 'networking' is about and how best to live and work ethically and effectively within a networked environment.

The Caring Economy is about attempting to give people a route map for a journey to a new age. It says to the business person "Do not be scared, do not over-react." Things are not going to be all that different. The digital age will be more than anything else about people communicating, interacting and trading with other people.

The Author:
GERRY MCGOVERN is the Managing Director of NUA, a Dublin-based Internet consultancy that has won many key US and international contracts.

320 pages
1-901657-61-2 hbk: May 1999
1-901657-60-4 pbk: December 1999

The Celtic Tiger:
From The Outside Looking In

May Valarasan-Toomey

This book looks at the social development of Ireland between 1967 and 1998, through the eyes of a Sri Lankan woman who has lived in the country for over 30 years. It looks at important social institutions such as the family, schools, and the church, and considers attitudes to race, religion and refugees, attitudes that seem to be changing in the light of the new found economic prosperity brought about in the 1990s, and known as "The Celtic Tiger".

The book highlights the author's deep concern for an Ireland that is currently at the crossroads - enjoying new found prosperity that is bringing economic benefits to many, but at the cost of losing essential parts of the Irish character, such as the welcoming, the hospitality, the generosity, for which the people of this country have been known for centuries. Looking back to the sixties and seventies, the authors recalls how easy it was for her to settle in Dublin, how she was immediately made to feel welcome, and how Ireland conferred on her a deep sense of identity and belonging which she had failed to see in her own country of birth. She describes the people at this time - their way of life, their sense of humour, their language, and their attitudes. The book goes on to consider all these issues as they have developed in the intervening thirty years, and also laments the sorry state of affairs surrounding the handling of the "newcomers" to Ireland, the refugees and asylum seekers, who, for the first time in the history of the nation are seriously challenging the ability of the Irish to take on the concept of multiculturalism and move into the millennium.

Ultimately, the book issues a warning - do not let the new economic prosperity in Ireland - which may be short-lived - change the fundamental character of the nation, a character known for its welcome, its caring and its compassion.

The Author:
MARY VALASARAN-TOOMEY came to live in Ireland in 1967. She is a freelance editor and lecturer.

160 pages
1-901657-74-1 pbk: £16.99, 1998
1-901657-21-3 hbk: £20, 1998

Individuals and Enterprise: Creating Entrepreneurs for the New Millennium through Personal Transformation

Colin Coulson-Thomas

Individuals and Enterprise - Creating Entrepreneurs for the New Millennium through Personal Transformation is the follow-up to Colin Coulson Thomas' stunning 1997 bestseller *The Future of the Organization* (published by Kogan Page).

The Future of the Organization looked at the change and transformation that has taken place in the typical organization in the last decade, and suggested how companies and organizations should adapt to ensure that they are not left behind as the business world gears up for the new millennium. This book takes up where that one left off, in that it addresses the consequences of the changing nature of businesses and organizations from an individual perspective. It considers the implications and opportunities facing individuals and what they need to do at different stages of their working life, either within an organization, or going it alone as an entrepreneur.

Challenges such as career uncertainty, globalization, new forms of working and even redundancy can be turned into exciting opportunities. It is a global world now, full of easy means of communication and full of opportunity. The time is right for individuals to express themselves and fulfil themselves more than ever before, and organizations need to support individual growth and harness individual talents if they are to hold on to the biggest and most valuable resource they have - their people. The book also identifies what organizations need to do to enable entrepreneurship to flourish and to support value and enterprise creation.

The Author:
COLIN COULSON-THOMAS is a seasoned business writer of guru status. Previous works include *The Future of the Organization* and *Transforming the Company* (both Kogan Page). He is already working on his next book, *The Shape of Things to Come*, which will be a futuristic appraisal of how business will develop in the new millennium, and will be published by Blackhall Publishing in October 1999.

320 pages
1-901657-71-X hbk: £27.50, April 1999
1-901657-76-0 pbk: £14.99, December 1999

Leadership Challenges
for Effective Management

Tesfa Gebremedhin & Peter Schaeffer

The nature of business management has changed significantly in recent years. While in the past, significant leadership responsibilities were only assigned to designated managers, today's flatter hierarchies require leadership from a greater number of employees. The interest in, and emphasis on, team-building and teamwork is another recent and interrelated change.

Leadership Challenges for Effective Management is aimed at individuals who are, for the first time, in a leadership position. It is also intended for use by students on business and MBA courses, as an introductory text. The book discusses the difference between a contemporary leader and a traditional leader, and how one's roles and responsibilities change when a leadership position is assumed. It goes on to deal with specific leadership and management skills including:

- decision making and problem solving;
- delegation and empowerment;
- the techniques of team building;
- conflict management;
- performance appraisal.

The book also considers the moral dimensions of leadership with specific reference to the problem of discrimination in management and the need for professional ethics in management. Overall, the book is a first class appraisal of how to develop an effective leadership strategy and how to become a superb business leader.

The Authors:
TESFA GEBREMEDHIN and **PETER SCHAEFFER** both lecture in the Division of Resource Management at West Virginia University.

224 pages
1-901657-82-5 hbk: £22.50, June 1999

The above books can be purchased at any good bookshop or direct from:
BLACKHALL PUBLISHING
26 Eustace Street
Dublin 2.
Telephone: +44 (0)1-677-3242; Fax: +44 (0)1-677-3243;
e-mail: blackhall@tinet.ie